THE FATE OF YOUR DATE

THE *Fate* OF YOUR *Date*

Divination for Dating, Mating, and Relating

✦ ✦ ✦

Stefanie Iris Weiss & Sherene Schostak

Illustrations by Irma

CHRONICLE BOOKS
SAN FRANCISCO

ACKNOWLEDGMENT

We are deeply indebted to all of our clients and friends for divine inspiration straight from the dating trenches. We'd also like to thank our fantastic editor, Jodi Davis, for her insight and wisdom.

Text copyright © 2006 by Stefanie Iris Weiss and Sherene Schostak.
Illustrations copyright © 2006 by Irma.

Library of Congress Cataloging-in-Publication Data available.

ISBN: 0-8118-4871-X

Manufactured in China

Designed by Viola Sutanto.

Distributed in Canada by Raincoast Books
9050 Shaughnessy Street
Vancouver, British Columbia V6P 6E5

10 9 8 7 6 5 4 3 2 1

Chronicle Books LLC
85 Second Street
San Francisco, California 94105

www.chroniclebooks.com

Dedication

✦ ✦ ✦

We dedicate this book to you, dear reader, in your
pursuit of true love. Your fate is waiting for you:
go forth and find it.

CONTENTS

INTRODUCTION

Divine Intervention

FROM DEEP IN THE TRENCHES OF THE DATING WARS, you, dear reader, have called to us. And after hearing one too many stories of found-and-immediately-lost love, tales of perfectly intelligent women losing their heads over a simple date, we decided to write this book. The stilettos, the perfume, and great conversation help you land those dates, of course. But when it comes to the front end of a potential relationship, nothing gets you answers faster than a little divination.

Before we get started, let's clear up a persistent myth: divination is not just the stuff of psychics, palmists, and astrologers born with elusive, exclusive "gifts." These diviners have simply worked hard to refine innate, subtle talents into usable practices. You also have gifts, darling; you've just been too busy creating your life to develop them. All of this stuff is not really as mystical as you might think. Simply put, our minds are extremely powerful, but most are not trained to grasp all the information that continuously bombards us on so many levels. Any quantum theorist will tell you the same thing. The stimuli we encounter each moment are far beyond what normal human cognition can comprehend. The truth is out there. The divinatory arts simply help us to see the unseen. And that ain't mystical; it's just plain smart.

The Fate of Your Date aims to demystify the mystical, and make the ancient practices practical, once and for all. We created this book as a one-stop divination source for all things dating; a compendium of the best of the metaphysical arts. Are you ready to get closer? Is your date? Will your potential mate call? Will you call first? As a sexy, single, and available fish that doesn't *need* a bicycle but wouldn't mind taking a nice ride on one, you need to know if you've got a catch of the day, week, or lifetime (or if you need to throw your date back and recast that line). The Fate of Your Date is here to help.

We understand that each crucial dating stage calls for its own approach, so for ease of use we've divided the book into three sections: before, during, and after the date. The "Before" section outlines astrology, numerology, and tarot to help you with the inevitable "Should I or shouldn't I" moment—you know, that instant in the bar or the coffee shop or online when you're sizing up your specimen. Once you decide to pursue the date, you can move on to the "During" section. Here you'll learn how to use divinatory arts such as palmistry and face reading while you're on the actual date. Find out whether a second date is worth your while, do a little bit of "getting to know you," and dabble in some Jungian symbol reading. Finally, the "After" section helps you size up the potential of a relationship with dream analysis, white magic, and psyche-divining. You can undertake each of these divinatory arts surreptitiously, or you can completely give up the New Age goods—each art can be practiced openly or on the down low. It's your choice.

Now, even though the book is broken up into "Before," "During," and "After" sections, we encourage you to mix it up. You can use the astrology chapter after your third or fourth date, or after your fifth year of marriage, for example. You can consult the "Spell Craft" chapter before the date, and apply some of the principles of white magic even before your doorbell has rung. Take your pick—use just one divinatory art or all of them at once. Reading this book will help you hone your intuition. That's one of the fundamentals of divination—getting your gut to do the dirty work, and letting your mind take a rest for once. Whether you're reading a palm, pulling a tarot card, or analyzing a recent dream, your instincts are where it's at.

Some folks believe that first impressions provide all the information we need about a person, that the initial energy exchange trumps all subsequent conversations, overtures, and courtship rituals. Since we humans are still far from using most of the gray matter we're born with, evolution still has a long way to go before we can effectively eliminate in the first ten seconds of a meeting those who will hurt, fail, and disappoint us. This is why everyone needs a divinatory tool-box to draw from. Welcome to your very own.

Section 1

BEFORE THE DATE

ASTROLOGY

Starlight, Star Bright

When you need to know what makes him tick, astrology gives you instant insight. The zodiac will tell you everything you need to know to create the perfect date, sign by sign.

CAVEAT

✦ ✦ ✦

In this chapter we focus on the traits of each sun sign, but everyone's chart is highly nuanced and individual. If you want to learn more about your date, you'll need to consider the placement of the moon, Venus, Mars, and the rising sign, among other things. Astrology is a science and art with endless permutations. If you're interested in knowing basically **everything** about someone you fancy, you need to get that person's exact birth data. That means date, time, and place. If things are going swimmingly, it shouldn't be a problem to obtain these details and get the lowdown with the help of a friendly astrologer. But beware — analyzing someone's chart in great depth prior to the very first date can have serious repercussions: it may cause you to run away screaming or fall madly in love, or it can simply kill the magic.

ASTROLOGY OFFERS LADIES ON THE MAKE FAR MORE THAN A CHEESY PICKUP LINE at the bar. Just knowing someone's sign can tell you volumes about what kind of specimen you're dealing with. It shortens the awkward "getting to know you" period, and it offers an instant and excellent profile of a current crush. With just a mere slice of a chart, it's as easy as pie to ensure a great date.

Why should you put stock in astrology? It's one of the oldest divinatory arts on the planet, it's accessible, and it works like a dream. Five thousand years of empirical data from the Mayans to the Chinese to the Babylonians have given modern denizens of the dating universe much information to mine. And it's still used across the globe today. In fact, Vedic astrology (five thousand years old and counting) is still commonly used in India for matchmaking and timing marriages. The Chinese continue to use astrology for health and wellness, and we savvy Westerners use it for just about everything.

Most people are familiar with simple sun-sign astrology, but it's a lot more complex than you might first imagine. From the perspective of earth, the sun, moon, and planets move through the various constellations, creating the potential for certain events to unfold in our lives. For instance, if you were born with your moon in the sign of Pisces, you'll be naturally psychic, no matter what sun sign you were born into. But while professional astrologers pore over natal charts covered with cryptic symbols, squiggles, and mathematical equations to predict future events, it's not altogether necessary for us to dig that deep. You can divine a good deal about a potential partner simply by knowing that person's birth date. You don't even need to know the year to use this nifty chapter.

Getting the Goods

First things first. How do you find out your intended's sign? This may be a tough one, especially if you've just met. A quick chat doesn't always supply the vital stats.

Want to keep your divination activities on the down low? It's possible to get astro data without giving away the metaphysical farm. Here are some tricks to getting someone's birth date, even if you just met five minutes ago:

1. **SIMPLY ASK, "HOW OLD ARE YOU?"** This is usually OK, but significantly older or younger people might not like it much. Use your intuition. Once you have the age you can easily segue to "Oh, so when's your birthday?"

2. **EMPLOY SEASONAL/METEOROLOGICAL SUBTERFUGE.** If it's summer, say, "It's so oppressively hot outside. I hate August. I prefer the fall, because that's when I was born. In October. What about you?"

3. **OUT WITH FRIENDS?** Say it's your pal's birthday, even if it's not. This works well: "Wish my friend X here a happy birthday! Oh, when's *your* birthday?"

4. **CELEBRITY BIRTHDAYS.** Look up who was born on that day before you step out for the evening, just in case. When you're chatting, casually ask, "Did you know that it's so-and-so's birthday? When's yours?"

5. **TAKE A GANDER AT YOUR POTENTIAL MATE'S DRIVER'S LICENSE.** Be coy. Or be blatant — "I'll show you mine if you show me yours."

6. **YOU CAN ALWAYS USE THE IRONICALLY CHEESY PATH TO GETTING THIS VITAL INFO**—just say "Hey, baby, what's your sign?"

Once you've got the birth date, you can consult this chart to divine the sun sign. (Note: These dates are just a tiny bit loose—in certain years the dates shift by a day or two, and some people are born on the cusp between signs, the day that the sign shifts. For these folks, it's best to consult an astrological ephemeris for the specific year of birth, available at your local New Age book shop, or easy to find online.)

ARIES {March 21 to April 20}

TAURUS {April 21 to May 20}

GEMINI {May 21 to June 20}

CANCER {June 21 to July 21}

LEO {July 22 to August 21}

VIRGO {August 22 to September 21}

LIBRA {September 22 to October 22}

SCORPIO {October 23 to November 21}

SAGITTARIUS {November 22 to December 20}

CAPRICORN {December 21 to January 18}

AQUARIUS {January 19 to February 17}

PISCES {February 18 to March 20}

Sign Language

Here's where you'll learn the nitty-gritty about your potential paramour. This section covers each sign's general personality profile, approach to romance, and physical intimacy style. We'll also show you what to expect on the actual date, how to handle the post-date wait, and your compatibility by sign. Whew!

ARIES (March 21 to April 20)

PERSONALITY PROFILE

The true firecracker cuties of the zodiac, Aries snap, crackle, and pop with more enthusiasm and raw energy than all the signs put together. They need to be the first to do, know, and try anything. So don't try to one-up them unless your idea of a good time is butting heads. Even the seemingly small and sweet ones are truly built tougher than a Ram truck.

APPROACH TO LOVE

Aries relish a chase, love to fight, live for the make-up sex afterward, and never take no for an answer. If they want you, they will grab you. If they aren't interested, trust us, you'll know. Don't forget that they are young tykes at heart and will pretty much kick and scream when they don't get their way. Try letting them win every now and again, and you'll have them for life.

THE DATE
What to wear: Wear either a red-hot siren dress or something so innocent and girlie that you look like jailbait. Spritz on some honeysuckle or peppermint. Where to go: Aries love both extremes. Suggest the hottest, latest scenester spots. They adore high-energy happenings that give a sense of exploring new territory, like race-car driving, dance parties, outdoor BBQs, and chasing you around. Change locations frequently, since Aries have very short attention spans. What to eat: Super-spicy foods (think cayenne pepper) or mushy, squishy baby foods that they don't have to chew much (chewing wastes time). Conversation: It's all about the Aries, so prepare to discuss their adventures and possibly get interrupted once in a while.

FOOLING AROUND
Giving it up: You must play hard to get with the Aries. Leave it at just a kiss good night. They love a challenge. Smooch style: Wildly intense and sometimes too much tongue. They're really, really into it.

POST-DATE
The call: Don't even consider waiting by the telephone. Aries won't wait to call if they like you. And don't call your

Aries. (See "Fooling Around" page 25.) Second date: What you see is what you get with Aries, so if you didn't like round one, you can pass on a second date.

MATCH MADE IN HEAVEN: *Gemini*

MATCH MADE IN HELL: *Capricorn*

*Go out with an Aries when the moon
is in Aries, Leo, Sagittarius, or Aquarius.*

TAURUS (April 21 to May 20)

PERSONALITY PROFILE

Walk softly but carry a big meal. Taurus is the meat-and-potatoes sign of the zodiac. Solid as a rock, these folks will stay hitched to their loyal mate for eons. So get your piece before it's too late. It will take more than a crowbar to pry them away from a relationship even if it's gone sideways. They hold on and on for dear life. Gentle as baby cows, they'll adore you as long as you don't push them or rearrange their furniture when they aren't looking

APPROACH TO LOVE

Once hooked, they're as steadfast as can be. But don't try to bully them into a love affair. Nothing turns them off faster than a push-and-shove approach to courtship. They like to feel as though they are in the driver's seat with you strapped in all safe and secure for as long as they want to possess you. They don't like to rush when it comes to anything, least of all love. They adore long dinners, long walks, and long kisses in the garden.

THE DATE

What to wear: Try soothing, earthy tones and lots of textures. Taureans relish all of their five senses, especially the tactile. They find lavender, rose, and grass scents intoxicating. Where to go: Sensual, natural, and classic locales with a solid feel please them most. Your Taurus won't want to share you, so don't suggest group outings. An ideal date might include eating, drinking, strolling through a garden, and scratch-and-sniff activities. Try a comfy, down-home restaurant with reliable food and big portions where you can take things slow and stay as long as you want. What to eat: Steak, spuds, and chocolate are favorite staples. Conversation: Discuss down-to-earth topics such as food, art, and best friends.

FOOLING AROUND

Giving it up: Don't play hard to get *too* hard. Just a tiny bit of push and pull is perfect for the sturdy Taurus. Smooch style: If you like long, leisurely, sensual smooches, you've found your match. Take it slow, light scented candles, and keep good-smelling foods handy—Taureans don't mind getting messy. They might keep sniffing you, but don't be put off; it's their way of connecting.

POST-DATE

The call: This is a super-slow sign, so don't expect an immediate phone call. We don't suggest making the first call after the date. This sign wants to be in control, so brace yourself for a wait. Second date: Even if the first date seemed a bit boring, give your Taurus another chance to blossom.

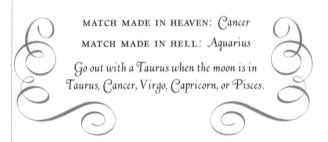

MATCH MADE IN HEAVEN: *Cancer*

MATCH MADE IN HELL: *Aquarius*

Go out with a Taurus when the moon is in Taurus, Cancer, Virgo, Capricorn, or Pisces.

GEMINI (May 21 to June 20)

PERSONALITY PROFILE

No one knows if they're coming or going (nor do they) and yet Gemini's whimsical ways are so alluring that you will happily chase them to and fro in order to find out what they're so busy running after. Obsessed with data and minutiae, they can talk up a storm.

APPROACH TO LOVE

To understand the attention span and fickle nature of a Gemini, think of a thirteen-year-old in love. Geminis are the teenagers of the zodiac. If you can tell good stories or make them laugh, they're hooked. But their restless and capricious ways will always make you wonder: Are you getting the real deal? Or encountering the Gemini's doppelganger, their shadow side?

THE DATE

What to wear: The latest. It's all about what's trendy for the Gemini. Tees with interesting phrases will delight them endlessly. You'll want to smell youthful and fresh—wear the latest pop star–inspired scent. Geminis also like orange blossom, spearmint, and tangerine. Where to go: Group activities are a good bet. Geminis are loath to get too intimate right away and friends can be a great buffer for them. Keep the date short, sweet, and light. Have a backup list of activities to keep this ADD-prone sign from getting bored. Suggest charades, board games, chess, and crossword puzzles. What to eat: Smoothies, any takeout, and kid's meals will satisfy the Gemini belly. Conversation: Keep changing subjects every three minutes and you'll have them hooked (maybe not for life, but for the next three minutes anyway, until you change the subject again). Read the newspaper that day so you can toss out savvy sound bites. Nothing charms a Gemini quite like a well-honed wit, so be at your alert best. Practice telling jokes and drink a cup of coffee before the date.

FOOLING AROUND

Giving it up: Be cunning but not too sly. Geminis like a little challenge. You'll definitely have fun with this sign, but beware of their fickle temperament and tendency to seek out the next big thing. Smooch style: They can be spazzy kissers, but we've found that some of them are total Don Juans; we suppose all that experience must breed perfection.

POST-DATE

The call: Geminis will likely call as long as they remember where they put your number and can find time while doing twelve other tasks. You can definitely make the first call after a date with this sign. They love nothing more than to gab away on the phone. Or, send them a quick e-mail. Instant messages turn them on big time. Second date: By all means, go for a second date even if you weren't totally dazzled the first time around. You need to see the other twin to really get a sense of the dual nature of a Gemini.

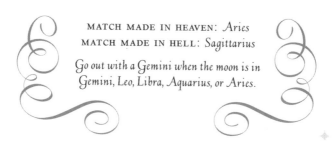

MATCH MADE IN HEAVEN: *Aries*
MATCH MADE IN HELL: *Sagittarius*

Go out with a Gemini when the moon is in Gemini, Leo, Libra, Aquarius, or Aries.

CANCER (June 21 to July 21)

PERSONALITY PROFILE

Here's the mushy, gushy home-lovin' sign of the zodiac. These folks are all about roots and family. Their moods change like the wind, but they will never stop caring about you. Just be careful not to hurt their feelings. Keep them happy by indulging in reveries of the past. Cancers are suckers for memories—they're the type who keep boxes of old journals, childhood photographs, and other reminders of meaningful moments close at hand at all times.

APPROACH TO LOVE

If they care for you, Cancers will mother you (or smother you if you're not careful). Prepare them a meal to find your way into their soft, adoring hearts. If you find out their favorite food on the first date and then serve it on the next, they'll start in with the "soul mate" thing before you can wash the dishes.

THE DATE

What to wear: Go for super feminine, goddess-inspired dresses. They like the scent of lily of the valley, honey, lilac, or chocolate milk. Where to go: Suggest flea markets (to browse antiques), or watch a movie. Even if you can't cook to save your life, scent the air with something that says you were born to be a happy homemaker. If they ask to cook you dinner, say yes (your Cancer catch is probably a born chef). At the very least, suggest a cozy and intimate restaurant.

What to eat: To really get a Cancer going, offer to cook dinner at your place. If you're culinarily inclined, serve apple pie à la mode, just like mom used to make. Meatloaf and cupcakes run a close second. Conversation: Talk about their past, family, and home. Cancers are shy, so avoid group activities.

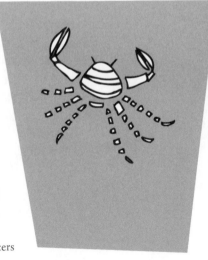

FOOLING AROUND

Giving it up: Their sincerity will make you feel safe and protected, so you don't have to worry about going too far. Smooch style: Cancers possess an instinctively mushy-gushy kissing style. The beauty of Cancers is that they're all about cuddling. If they pay particular attention to your breasts, don't get freaked out. They *loooove* soft curves.

POST-DATE
The call: Because they hate to hurt anyone's feelings, Cancers will probably call you either way. But because they're slightly shy, it's more than OK for you to make the first post-date call. It could take some of the pressure off. Second date: Cancers are usually softies inside a hard shell. Give them another chance to warm up and show you their loony sense of humor, since their natural shyness may have subdued it the first time around.

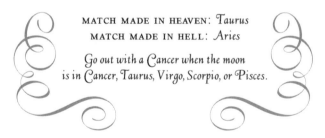

MATCH MADE IN HEAVEN: *Taurus*
MATCH MADE IN HELL: *Aries*

Go out with a Cancer when the moon is in Cancer, Taurus, Virgo, Scorpio, or Pisces.

LEO (July 22 to August 21)

PERSONALITY PROFILE
The hotshot showstoppers of the zodiac, Leos have made an art of getting others to adore them and follow their lead.

They're born performers. Even if they're not acting for a living, they live to act. With Leos, there is no such thing as too much flattery. Bestow a few choice compliments and you'll have them eating right out of your hand. They have gigantic hearts and will spoil you rotten.

APPROACH TO LOVE

Leos adore courting their object of affection. If they've got the hots for you, they'll make no bones about letting you know; look forward to lots of affection and/or gifts. They also expect to be treated like God's gift to dating. Prepare to shower them with compliments if you want to hear them purr. Know that they take offense when you look around the room at other people—they must be the center of attention at all times—so keep your eyes from wandering if you want to keep that Leo happy.

THE DATE

What to wear: Dress like a rock star or runway model. You can't overdo it. They love the drama! Go for a citrusy scent, since orange and lemon drive them crazy. Where to go: Check out any local red carpet scenes. Go for see-and-be-seen locales where luxury and glamour abound. Or just go and sit in the sun somewhere. This sign will not share the limelight, so don't recommend group activities for the first date. What to eat: Suggest restaurants fit for royalty. Champagne and caviar are excellent food choices. Conversation: If you shower nonstop compliments on your Leo, the date is likely to last a long, long time. Be dramatic, but don't cut into the Leo's monologue.

FOOLING AROUND

Giving it up: Play a little hard to get, but don't forget to adore the Leo at the same time. You cannot be expressive enough with a Leo. It's an art. Smooch style: These are the professional makeout artists of the zodiac—some of the best kissers, hands down.

POST-DATE

The call: Leos can't resist flattery, so go ahead and call first. Second date: They only get more dramatic with time, so if you didn't love their histrionics during date one, you might find them annoying the second time around.

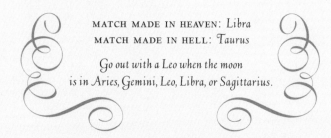

MATCH MADE IN HEAVEN: *Libra*
MATCH MADE IN HELL: *Taurus*

*Go out with a Leo when the moon
is in Aries, Gemini, Leo, Libra, or Sagittarius.*

VIRGO (August 22 to September 21)

PERSONALITY PROFILE

They may fuss a bit and worry a lot, but Virgos know how
to take care of you, down to every last cotton-pickin' detail.
Born to play nurse (male or female), they will make sure you
take your vitamins, eat three square meals a day, and get a
full eight hours. Perfection is their primary goal and it can
also be their undoing. They can be neat freaks, and they
adore every creature in the animal kingdom.

APPROACH TO LOVE

Virgos can be a bit cautious and critical when it comes to
choosing a date or mate — they tend to look for perfection
(or at least perfect
hygiene). On the other
hand, they sometimes
throw discretion to
the wind. Once they've
decided they can fit
dating into their schedule
or that they've had enough
solitude, they will work
on trying to perfect themselves for you.

THE DATE

What to wear: Keep it simple, silly. Make sure you
look clean and put together:

no wrinkles or unsightly seams, please. The more tailored and pressed, the better. (Do consider wearing very naughty undergarments, though, and letting one stray strap peek through at key moments. However, this does not mean that you should wear lowriders with your panties sticking out. Never, ever do this with a Virgo, or you'll risk causing a panic attack.) Wear White Linen, bathe with Ivory soap, or apply other subtle, almost nondetectable scents. The idea is to smell clean and mild. Where to go: Suggest anything intellectually stimulating but make sure it's in good taste. Health food and vitamin shopping is fun for them, or perhaps a yoga class. They will definitely arrive on time, so don't be late. No group activities for this sign on a first date. They have a hard enough time leaving the soothing solitude of their homes to go on the date in the first place. What to eat: Go for healthy and light. Wherever you eat, make sure it's clean. Conversation: Virgos love to critique, analyze, and break things down into their myriad parts in a hundred different ways, so be ready for an involved discussion.

FOOLING AROUND

Giving it up: Don't play hard to get, because Virgos will analyze it for hours, worry themselves to death, and give up on you in the process. However, proper, ladylike behavior will go a long way on the first date. Play up the purity factor, with a hint that there may be a naughty side lurking behind that coy demeanor. A quick kiss at the door is fine. Smooch style: If things go further, you don't have to worry about receiving a slobbery kiss. They aim to please in a very refined way.

POST-DATE

The call: After analyzing every detail of the evening and deciding that it is a practical thing to do, a Virgo will call, and at precisely the right moment. We don't suggest calling first — it might annoy. Second date: If you had a good mental connection, give the Virgo another twirl. It takes a few dates for a Virgo to loosen up.

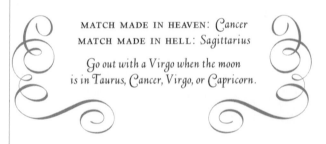

MATCH MADE IN HEAVEN: *Cancer*
MATCH MADE IN HELL: *Sagittarius*

Go out with a Virgo when the moon
is in Taurus, Cancer, Virgo, or Capricorn.

LIBRA (September 22 to October 22)

PERSONALITY PPROFILE

If you dig pretty packaging and a strong intellect, you have met your match in Libra. Good thing, because they're always searching for *their* perfect match. They need to complete themselves — it's their raison d'être. Sure, they have an impossible time making up their mind and will drag you into their own hemming-and-hawing world, but they are so sweet and dangerously charming that you'll think you're having fun in the land of the lost. These are the true diplomats of the zodiac.

APPROACH TO LOVE

Diehard romantics, Libras spend their lives searching for their soul mate. The only problem is they're often terrified of commitment because it involves making a major decision. They like having options. Once they do finally decide on some-one, though, that's it. They will make your world beautiful.

THE DATE

What to wear: Go for that perfect blend of masculine and feminine when it comes to dressing. Libras are all about elegance and great taste. They appreciate the classics. Jasmine, rose, and freesia turn them on. Where to go: Libras love art openings, museum exhibits, fine din-ing, tasteful parties, and hand-holding.

Going for dessert will also please. Suggest places with beautiful ambience. Don't give them too many options, though; this will upset their quest for equilibrium. What to eat: Haute cuisine, beautifully arranged on elegant china and perfectly balanced in color and shape, makes them happiest. Conversation: Discuss relationships, politics, or art, or engage in a healthy debate. Libras feel more at ease in social situations and have fewer decisions to make when others are involved, so group activities work well for this sign.

FOOLING AROUND
Giving it up: Definitely play hard to get, and make them think they have competition. They can't stand not being the chosen one. Libras are charmers but the most fickle of all the signs. Make sure you don't go too far before they've had a chance to make up their mind about you. (This might take a while.) Smooch style: The Libran kissing style is too good to be true unless, of course, they can't decide whether they are going to kiss you or not and end up smashing noses with you as a result.

POST-DATE
The call: Notoriously wishy-washy, Libras may not have the ability to call right away. It's easy to drive yourself crazy waiting for this sign to call. And the kicker is that we don't suggest that you call first, because it might freak them out in the midst of their delicate decision-making process. Second date: Go for seconds given the opportunity, but do watch out for their disarming charm. It's easy to fall in love with a Libra.

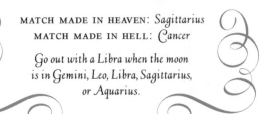

MATCH MADE IN HEAVEN: *Sagittarius*
MATCH MADE IN HELL: *Cancer*

Go out with a Libra when the moon is in Gemini, Leo, Libra, Sagittarius, or Aquarius.

SCORPIO (October 23 to November 21)

PERSONALITY PROFILE

Scorpios. Their reputations precede them. They are intense and passionate and always live a little too close to the edge. They prefer to keep their own skeletons in the closet, so don't get too nosy. If they seem mild mannered or shy at first, don't let the cool exterior fool you. A volcano smolders within. Date at your own risk.

APPROACH TO LOVE

Scorpios can't take anything lightly, especially love. It's all or nothing. They will go to Hades and back to win your affection. But if they decide it's over, they'll make it crystal clear. You will feel like they've died.

THE DATE

What to wear: Choose miniskirts, black leather pants, hip huggers, or low-slung jeans. Black and burgundy are favorite colors. Girly girls with an edge get props. It's OK to look like a bit of a slutty schoolgirl when you're

with a Scorpio. They like tuberose and sandalwood scents.
Where to go: Dark corners of bars, underground scenes, and
sexy lounges thrill them. The actual date should be either
super long or super short, depending on how much intensity
you can handle. They love extremes and won't tolerate anything halfway. Do not suggest group activities under any
circumstances. Scorpios are naturally possessive and won't
go for this. What to eat: Delight them with red wine,
whiskey, and dark chocolate. Conversation: They love to
talk about anything you're not supposed to talk about.
Things could get deep.

FOOLING AROUND
Giving it up: At first, play hard to get, and do it with as much
mystery as you can muster. But hold on to your britches!
It will be difficult not to go far with this mesmerizing and
sexual creature. Beware the hypnotizing eyes. Smooch style:
These passionate, smoldering kissers will knock you off your
feet by figuring out exactly what you like best. We're
getting weak in the knees just thinking about it.

POST-DATE
The call: A Scorpio who gets obsessed might call twelve
times instead of just once. You can call first, but play it cool.
Second date: You'll need seconds, thirds, and fifths to get
to the bottomless bottom of this deep and complex creature.
Try again. And again.

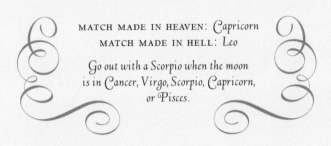

SAGITTARIUS (November 22 to December 20)

PERSONALITY PROFILE

Here is the born philosopher, world traveler, and wise sage
all wrapped up into one fun-loving package. If you need
a positive energy charge, stick with a Sag. These people have
enough faith to keep the rest of us going. They will crack
you up but if you can't take brutal honesty you might want
to reconsider. This lot tells it like it is.

APPROACH TO LOVE

Sagittarians treat love like an adventure to be experienced
to the fullest. They're forever optimistic that the most failing
relationship will somehow work out. But often they're most
in love with the open road, so if you want to stay in their
good graces, prepare for a journey.

THE DATE

What to wear: Sporty, athletic looks earn big points. Bright
colors and bold looks are surefire picks. Go for fun and

43

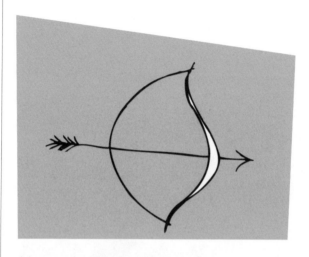

uplifting scents or exceptionally exotic fragrances like
Moroccan rose or Indian jasmine. Where to go: Suggest sky-
diving, horseback riding, checking out the latest guru or
motivational speaker, or jetting to an exotic subcontinent.
When the fun factor starts to fizzle, call it a night. Sagittarian
boredom is hard to miss; in fact, you'll probably know immediately, as they begin to look around the room for something
more intriguing. Change locations frequently, as the Sag
always fears missing out on something over there, where
that greener grass is growing. What to eat: Suggest the
most exotic foods from the nether regions of the continent.
Conversation: Philosophy, religion, and comedy are their
topics of choice. Group activities are mighty fine — they
sure do love a party!

FOOLING AROUND

Giving it up: Play hard to get—Sagittarians love healthy competition. They won't judge you if some of your clothes come off, but remember that these folks are a bit fickle. Keep it challenging (again, think sports). Smooch style: Blessed with all kinds of other gifts, Sagittarians can be a bit clumsy in the kissing department. Your feet could get stepped on and stuff might get knocked over, but who the hell cares when you're swept up in the moment?

POST-DATE

The call: The Sag will likely call you right away, to let you know the truth about the date. You can make the first call, though, because Sagittarians are nothing if not broad-minded. Second date: Sagittarians are pretty much open books, so if the first date didn't go so well, don't expect anything different the second time around.

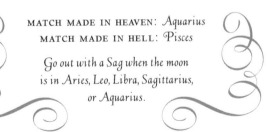

MATCH MADE IN HEAVEN: *Aquarius*
MATCH MADE IN HELL: *Pisces*

Go out with a Sag when the moon is in Aries, Leo, Libra, Sagittarius, or Aquarius.

CAPRICORN (December 21 to January 18)

PERSONALITY PROFILE
Capricorns embody status, worldliness, and high standards. They are practical as all get-out, so don't try to impress them with anything flimsy or fleeting or trendy. They want quality and only go first-class. They really care about credentials — so losers, slackers, and underachievers need not apply. Pillars of strength, they meet every challenge they're given. If you're looking for somebody to look up to, choose a Capricorn.

APPROACH TO LOVE
These folks are super-sensible and a bit conservative when it comes to everything, including romance. For them, love is kinda like a business transaction. They measure out time invested against rewards gained. They won't waste time on love if they aren't seriously interested; they've got better things to do, like finish their nineteenth degree and get to their third job. But they'll take you seriously, too, which can be quite a commodity, don't you think?

46

THE DATE

What to wear: Keep your style conservative but don't be afraid to experiment with looks that suggest power and status. If you look like a million bucks no matter what your bank balance, you'll have it in the bag. Understated classic scents are what work—or the most expensive perfume you can buy. Where to go: Suggest high-end entertainment. A sophisticated cabaret act, a stellar movie premiere, and a five-star restaurant make for excellent choices. Go for broke. The perfect nightcap is a dry martini in a class-act nightclub. Caps find it tacky to bring any tagalongs, so let it be just the two of you. What to eat: If they let you make a restaurant suggestion (not terribly likely), choose joints that feature excellent prime rib and an extensive wine list. Conversation: Discuss business, money, politics, and discipline, and your Capricorn's latest big accomplishment.

FOOLING AROUND

Giving it up: To seduce a randy Capricorn, act cool, calm, and detached yet entirely sincere. Think old-fashioned and hold to your boundaries when it comes to jumping into bed. Smooch style: They're good kissers but may be reserved at first. Their talents come from having studied well.

POST-DATE

The call: If you're a high priority, a Capricorn will call you. You should probably wait for your Cap to call, since they're sort of old school. If you don't get a call, your date may have already written you off. Second date: Believe your first impressions. If you found the Cap too conservative the first time, it's unlikely he or she will suddenly loosen up and go wild.

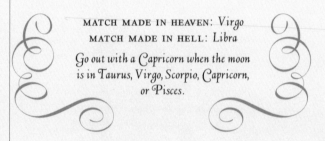

MATCH MADE IN HEAVEN: *Virgo*
MATCH MADE IN HELL: *Libra*

Go out with a Capricorn when the moon is in Taurus, Virgo, Scorpio, Capricorn, or Pisces.

AQUARIUS (January 19 to February 17)

PERSONALITY PROFILE

These genius folks are all about experimenting and breaking out of the box. You may not realize how eccentric they are until you really get to know them. At first, they may seem oddly detached and curious, as if they're conducting a science project. In actuality, they're searching for their new best friend.

APPROACH TO LOVE

If you have goals in common with them, Aquarians get really excited. They're impressed by anyone who dares to be different and doesn't give a fig what others think about them. Embrace your inner weirdo and you will be a magnet for their affections. It's also essential that their friends like you. "The more the merrier" applies when it comes to dating

Aquarians. They really get turned on when you invite them to hang out with you and your posse. Their air of detachment can be terrifying to more clingy types, but they will be the best friend you ever have.

THE DATE

What to wear: Aquarian taste runs the gamut from ultra - conservative to crazy hippie to ultramodern. They wear their freak flags high, and so should you. The weirder the better. It's OK to go synthetic with Aquarians. Try an off-the-wall futuristic scent. Or just wear essential oil of violet, their birth flower. Where to go: Suggest stargazing or tribal dance parties. What to eat: To keep experimental Aquarians on their toes, recommend

the most bizarre cuisine you can imagine, and order things you've never risked before — like the potentially poisonous puffer fish at the chic Japanese restaurant that just opened in your city. Conversation: Talk about the future, science fiction, astrology, astral travel, and Einstein.

FOOLING AROUND

Giving it up: If you treat the Aquarian like a buddy, even in the heat of passion, they'll go mad for you. Only problem is that they might consider you their next science experiment, and not everyone can deal with being the subject of such scrutiny. Smooch style: Their kissing technique can border on kinky — but often, it's just plain good.

POST-DATE

The call: Aquarians will want to be friends no matter what, so a post-date call is likely, even if you had little romantic chemistry. This sign has no trouble with others taking the initiative to make the first call, so if you want, go for it. Second date: An Aquarius will expand your world, so give the date a second and third chance even if you don't click right away. Sometimes testing takes time.

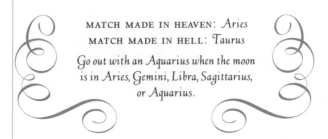

MATCH MADE IN HEAVEN: *Aries*
MATCH MADE IN HELL: *Taurus*

Go out with an Aquarius when the moon is in Aries, Gemini, Libra, Sagittarius, or Aquarius.

PISCES (February 18 to March 20)

PERSONALITY PROFILE

The oh-so-compassionate hearts of the zodiac, Pisces are forever drowning in the collective chaos. If you can get these people to answer the phone, you will have made major headway. Deeply spiritual, they will worship at the altar of their latest crush. Dating is a religious experience and they will bear any cross to get you to merge with them. They truly don't know where you end and they begin.

APPROACH TO LOVE
Boundaries, shmoundaries. These softies want to drown in the wonder that is you. There is nothing they won't do to make the connection happen. But if you are too pushy or not passionate enough they might quickly swim away. Make sure you love to sleep, because these fish can't get enough zzz's. They definitely prefer to be unconscious whenever possible.

THE DATE
What to wear: Wear the most dreamy color and fabric combinations you can find. Romantic, mystical gypsy clothes make Pisces swoon. Spritz on some aquatic-themed perfume, or just dab some saltwater behind the ear. Where to go: Suggest swimming, sailing, dancing, movies, nightclubs, temples, concerts, seascapes, poetry readings, and spiritual gatherings. Don't bring a Pisces on a group date the first time around, because it will just cause confusion. They feel "vibes," and too many personalities can overwhelm these folks. There

is no end and no beginning for a Pisces, so you'll probably have to say good night first. As you can imagine, first dates with Pisces often turn into sleepovers. What to eat: They adore wine sauces, heavenly desserts, and, sometimes, too many glasses of wine. You'll want to keep tabs on their alcohol consumption. Conversation: Talk about mysticism, poetry, your dream journal, and anything spiritual.

FOOLING AROUND

Giving it up: Be careful, because Pisces can convince you of almost anything, like the idea that sleeping with them immediately will be good for your soul. Try to wait, because if it happens, it's likely to be both beautiful and meaningful. Smooch style: You've found the most divine kisser of the zodiac. You'll feel as if you're being transported to heaven.

POST-DATE

The call: Even if a Pisces likes you, this fish may be hiding under the covers dreaming about you instead of dialing you up. Should you make the first call? Absolutely. The Pisces *needs* you. Second date: Still waters run deep. To find out what's swimming beneath the surface, you'll need a few more dates.

MATCH MADE IN HEAVEN: *Scorpio*
MATCH MADE IN HELL: *Gemini*

*Go out with a Pisces when the moon
is in Taurus, Cancer, Scorpio, Capricorn,
or Pisces.*

# Sunshine of Your Love

Whenever possible, start your dating divination with astrology. It's the perfect platform from which to dive into the rest of the divinatory arts, and it will give you the most comprehensive overview of your date's personality, potential quirks, and general dateability. Don't dump anyone just because that person is not your most compatible match—the sun sign doesn't tell the whole story. Just use your wiles to hit your date in those vulnerable planetary soft spots. Go ahead. We give you permission.

NUMEROLOGY

By the Numbers

Will this date compute? Sum up the potential with a bit of numerology. You don't even need a calculator.

Everything is numbers and to know numbers is to know thyself.

——PYTHAGORAS

Mathematics, rightly viewed, possesses not only truth, but supreme beauty.

——BERTRAND RUSSELL,
The Study of Mathematics

IF LIFE AND DATING WERE AS SIMPLE AS A MATHE-
MATICAL EQUATION, maybe we'd all have it figured out
by now. You know, $1 + 1 = 2$. Well, kiddies, we have
some stellar news for you. When you unlock the simple
secrets of numerology, your dating life will really add up
to something.

One of the basic precepts of *The Fate of Your Date* is that
energy is everything. Unfortunately, from day one we're
taught that physical reality can't be transcended. To some
degree this is true, but just because you can't walk through
walls doesn't mean that you can't harness and manipulate
energy. And numbers are merely energy. It's true. Numerology is simply the study of numbers and their symbolic

significance — their energy. Each number has its own unique vibration and meaning.

Numerology's roots lie in several ancient traditions. You'll find references to numerology in the Jewish mystical tradition of Kabbalah, and in African, Egyptian, Babylonian, Chinese, and Tibetan divination. It was famously used by an ancient Greek mathematician. Remember that pesky Pythagorean theorum? Well, we have wise old Pythagoras to thank for that.

Contemporary Western numerology is based on the system he developed, although it's evolved quite a bit since our old friend Pyth roamed the earth. Numerology fell out of favor in the West for quite some time, but interest in it picked up again in the good old days of the twentieth century, and modern metaphysicians rely on it heavily.

 Common Denominator

If you think of numbers as symbolic representations of energy or vibrations, you'll understand much better how to use them in daily life. In numerology, numbers are as consequential as matter. Our relationship to the numbers in our life is not at all arbitrary. Their energy is subtle but extremely power-ful. Because human beings have practiced numerology for thousands of years and in myriad cultures, the meanings of numbers have been ingrained in our collective unconscious and, quite possibly, our DNA. We may not understand intellectually what numbers signify, but deep in our core we know exactly what they mean.

Every modern numerologist has a slightly different approach, but we've developed a special dating divination methodology for you so you can dip your sticky little fingers into the cosmic cookie jar. All you need is your birth date, and your date's birth date, of course.

1 + 1 = 2, or Hey, Baby, What's Your Number?

You don't need to be a master of calculus to figure out your personal number. It's quite simple. Just add up the numbers in your birth date and then reduce them to a single digit (see below). Start with the actual day (single digits stay the same, double digits get added together). Next, add this figure to the number for the month of your birth. Then reduce the year of your birth to a single digit by adding those four numbers together. Finally, add these two figures together. You'll get a single digit (except in the case of master numbers; see page 63). This digit is considered your personal number. For example, if your birth date were April 14, 1971, the calculation would look like this:

Add the digits of the birth date (14): 1 + 4 = 5

Add the month (4) to the above figure: 5 + 4 = 9

Then add together the four digits of the year
of birth: 1 + 9 + 7 + 1 = 18

Reduce this to one digit: $1 + 8 = 9$

Then add together the two numbers for the date and month and the year: $9 + 9 = 18$

Reduce this to one digit (if you get a two-digit number, just add those two digits together until you have a single digit): $1 + 8 = 9$

Here's another example for July 19, 1980.

$$7 + 1 + 9 + 1 + 9 + 8 + 0 = 35$$

$$3 + 5 = 8$$

NAME GAME

✦ ✦ ✦

Another oft-used branch of modern numerology is a system in which the letters of the alphabet and their corresponding numbers are used to determine the meaning of one's name. This system, fundamental to Kabalistic numerology, is called Gematria. Just ask Madonna, or, ahem, Esther.

The personal number for the first example is nine. (See page 21 for tips on getting someone's birth information on the down low. If you don't have the actual birth date, you can also calculate a personal number just from the year of birth. For instance, 1968 would be $1 + 9 + 6 + 8 = 24$ and $2 + 4 = 6$. So you have a birth year 6 on your hands. This number reflects a generational tendency, but it still works well.)

The personal birth-date number represents one's potential, and the soul's goal this lifetime. But every day of the year also has a number. Figure out the number for the day you first encountered your intended, and calculate the number for your scheduled date. The results can be very telling.

One Is the Loveliest Number

Don't be fooled into thinking that your personal number (or your date's number, for that matter) is the be-all and end-all of your personality. We're talking potential here, nothing written in stone. Because numerology is endlessly complex and so many other factors are at play, these numbers should be looked at as merely a jumping-off point. Remember that your specimen is also in a particular numerological year right now. That means your date's personal number (and yours, too) is affected by current conditions. You can determine the number for the current year (called the "personal year") by adding it to the birth numbers, as discussed above. Use the same method of reduction to get a final number that suggests the nature of the current year.

The Numbers Game: What Your Digits Mean

1 Pioneering, creative, energetic; shows leadership qualities; can be selfish and dictatorial — 5, 7

2 Diplomatic, trustworthy, loyal; can be sensitive and gullible — 6, 8

3 Communicative, pleasure seeking, generous; can be scatterbrained and impractical — 7, 9

4 Responsible, reliable, disciplined; can be impatient and overly dominant — 8, 2

5 Magnetic, friendly, passionate; can be indecisive and hyperactive — 9, 1

6 Philosophical, intuitive, generous; can be jealous and argumentative — 2, 4

7 Sensitive, perceptive, spiritual; can be cold and secretive — 1, 3

8 Intelligent, confident, determined; can be intolerant and unforgiving — 4, 6

9 Broad-minded, intuitive, happy-go-lucky; can be selfish and resentful — 3, 5

Planning an event or reflecting on a past date? If you're calculating the number for a particular day, think of the above numbers as reflecting the personality of the day, or your or your date's temperament on that day.

Mastery

To add to your math homework, we have some additional numbers for you to crunch. Numbers 11 and 22 are considered to be extra, extra special. If a birth date adds up to an 11 or a 22, do not reduce it to a single digit. These two numbers possess a certain intensity—they pack a mighty numerological wallop. Both 11 and 22 indicate a passionate personality—for better and for worse. Eleven is the most intuitive of all the numbers. It is extremely sensitive, a number for dreamers, representing insight without rational thought. There's an artistic bent to this number that can indicate either greatness or a great fall from grace. Twenty-two is considered the most practical and ambitious of all the numbers. It's down-to-earth, allowing the person to turn fantasies into realities. Achievement is the prime motivation for the 22; and they'll go the extra mile to get what they want, although they can also be ambitious to the point of exhaustion and depression.

Summing It Up

Numerology has myriad applications. We all seem to be attracted or repelled by certain numbers. Often a special number will pop up over and over in our lives. Some report waking at the same time each morning sans alarm clock, getting the same amount of change on a regular basis, or moving into houses with the same numerical address over and over. These recurring relationships with numbers should add some

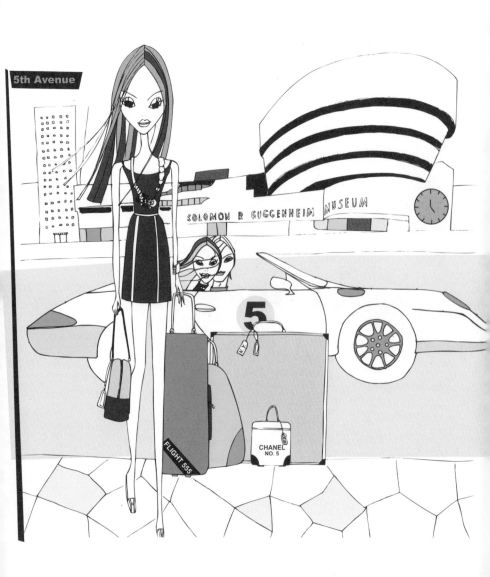

depth to your numerological understanding. Look up the meaning of any numbers that recur often—the universe may be trying to give you a message. Notice the time of day that your date calls to ask you out, add together the digits of your intended's phone number, and the number (address and phone) of the venue to which your date takes you. All of these numbers have significance. Refer to the chart on page 62 for insight into their meanings.

TAROT

It's in the Cards

Wondering what your date's vibe will be like tonight?
A Tarot reading will tell you what's on deck.

YOU'RE DRESSED AND READY TO GO. You look hot, if you do say so yourself. So what's the last thing you should do before slipping out the door to meet your date? Draw a tarot card, of course. A tarot reading, even a slapdash one, can divine some instant and valuable information. Like a high-powered microscope, the cards serve as a way to see what's going on deep inside your head and heart. The cards can tell you what you want, what you're ready for, and what you might encounter with your next conquest. Like cigarettes or a cocktail, they can also calm your nerves, although they're far healthier (but possibly just as addictive).

Tarot has been around for ages. The cards were first seen in the fifteenth century in northern Italy, when they were used for Triumphs, a game similar to bridge. A few centuries later occultists in France rediscovered the cards and began to use them for divinatory purposes. The images on tarot cards are said to be linked to Kabbalah, the ancient Jewish mystical sect favored by the Hollywood elite. Kabbalah is at least five thousand years old, as aged as the Hebrews of the Old Testament. It reflects the esoteric, spiritual side of Judaism.

Despite their storied past, tarot readings are not just the stuff of fortune-tellers with bad moles and ugly kerchiefs.

You can do readings yourself, in the privacy of your own home, and achieve expertise with enough practice. The power of tarot comes from the diviner (the reader) and the subject (if you're reading for yourself, that's you and you). The cards themselves don't possess any inherent magic. Instead, they serve as an intuitive tool. The very subtle energies passed between the reader and the subject reveal any unconscious, prescient knowledge about the question asked. You thought that you didn't know the answer, and you needed to *ask* the cards, did you? Well, that's not exactly how it works. The cards just show you what you already know but don't know that you know. Get it?

If you've never seen a deck, you're in for a treat. Tarot cards are beautiful and mysterious, full of ancient, archetypal images from throughout the ages. The images are so powerful that the cards make perfect meditation tools. Tarot decks should be wrapped in silk when not in use.

TIP: *We recommend the Rider-Waite deck. You can find it in just about any bookstore, or you can order one online. It's the best starter deck of all.*

Spreading Things Out

You'll find seventy-eight cards, made up of twenty-one major arcana and fifty-seven minor arcana, in your trusty tarot deck. A traditional tarot card reading draws from the entire deck. An excellent spread for newbies is the Celtic Cross (see diagram on facing page). (A "spread" is an expression for the various ways in which one can lay out the cards on the table.) But for a quick-and-dirty dating divination reading, you can simply work with the twenty-one major arcana. When you get a bit more sophisticated and/or curious, you can learn more about the rest of your deck by consulting the handy booklet that came with the deck or by picking up one of the great books suggested on page 159. For the spreads described here, you must first separate the twenty-one major arcana from the minor arcana. You can easily pull out the proper cards according to their titles, listed on the following pages under "Interpretations."

The Drive-Through, Single Card Reading

This reading is the perfect thing if you're running late and your date's at the door. The major arcana cards should be shuffled, laid facedown, and spread out in a fan. Close your eyes, take a deep breath, and meditate briefly on what you hope your date will bring. Then draw one card for an instant reading. See the interpretations that follow.

The Fate of Your Date Spread: A Five-Course Meal

If you've got a little time and want something a bit more complex, try this five-card spread. We've based this spread on general readings created by master tarot readers, but have tailored it a bit for our dating divination purposes.

As you did in the single card reading, you should shuffle the twenty-one cards while breathing deeply and focusing on the date. Then remove the top five cards one by one, spreading them out in a fan, face up. Read them from left to right. Position One shows the present moment, Position

Two represents the near future. Position Three signifies what's going on with you, and Position Four represents what's going on for your date. The final card symbolizes the outcome of the date and potential for a relationship.

 Interpretations

THE FOOL
Take a leap into the unknown. This card indicates that you're ready to start a new chapter when it comes to love and relationships. It calls for an open mind, a free heart, and a spontaneous attitude. It's OK to wear your heart on your sleeve. Anything can happen, and you're definitely going to learn something new.

THE MAGICIAN
Beware of the trickster. This card might reveal a clever character prone to using tricks to get what he wants. Communication is paramount, so keep your ears peeled and stay alert.

THE HIGH PRIESTESS
The Goddess force is with you. Trust your intuition, because that vibe is right-on. This card suggests that your feminine instincts remain strong and you're one with your womanly powers.

THE EMPRESS

Venus is the dominant energy of the Empress card. It's a card of pregnancy (don't take this too literally, but do use protection if you end up in bed), suggesting the situation is pregnant with possibility. Anything can happen.

THE EMPEROR

Someone may want to play boss. Watch out for power plays and be sure to hold your own. Self-possession is key.

THE HIGH PRIEST

This card indicates a need to keep the faith despite what you may see or hear. If you truly listen on a deeper level, you will understand the spiritual or inspirational connection at hand.

THE LOVERS

Looking for love at first sight? Off-the-hook chemistry? You may have just found it. The Lovers card symbolizes a union of the opposites, a yin-yang coming together of pieces that fit perfectly.

THE CHARIOT

This card can foretell a beautiful merger. But if the timing is off you may find yourself feeling unusually emotional about lost potential. In any case, a lot of feelings are bound to come up in the near future.

STRENGTH
This card calls for an extra shot of self-confidence. Don't be afraid to put your head in the lion's mouth, so to speak. Just make sure the lion doesn't bite: keep your lust in check.

THE HERMIT
This card symbolizes solitude and the need to stay close to home. Meditation and retreat are indicated.

WHEEL OF FORTUNE
A lucky break is in store and you're in for quite a ride. This card suggests an excessively good time — too much is not enough. But one too many spins might make you dizzy, so go easy.

JUSTICE
Keep a cool head and don't jump to any conclusions. It's best to take the middle path. The more you take a rational, rather than emotional, approach to matters, the better off you'll be.

DEATH

A very intense, transformative experience may lie ahead. You might not know what just hit you, but you'll welcome it again. The Death card also indicates the potential for a strong magnetic connection guaranteed to take you to new heights or new depths. You'll think you've died and gone either to heaven or to the underworld.

TEMPERANCE

Listen carefully to your inner voice. Avoid extremes and keep one foot on the ground at all times. You may feel that your guardian angels are floating above, making your wishes come true—and you may be right.

THE DEVIL

Temptation. Degradation. Sexual obsession. Need we say more? Try not to become overly consumed by passion and don't let fear, shame, or lust get the best of you. We recommend not taking off your clothes if you draw this card.

THE HANGED MAN

Try to be OK with the nebulous quality of this card. It's

ROLE REVERSAL

✦ ✦ ✦

When laying out your cards face up for a reading, you may end up placing some upside down. Tarot experts have multiple approaches to reading upside-down, or reversed, cards. Some readers make sure all of their cards are facing the same direction every time they lay out their cards to avoid any possible reversals. Others say that when cards are laid out upside down, the opposite of the card's meaning is invoked. For your first readings, we suggest you keep things straight up. All it takes is a careful reordering of your cards after each reading.

not supposed to point to a definitive outcome. Tolerate the interesting chaos—you may have a major epiphany as a result of sitting with uncertainty.

THE TOWER
Expect a radical shift of perception, almost as if your whole world has been shaken up at its core. You may experience a strange new sense of liberation.

THE STAR

Your wish has come true. You may feel like you have just
met your new best friend as waves of calm and tranquility
wash over you from the get-go. Enjoy all that you have
in common and your amazing instant connection.

THE SUN

Here comes the fun. Be totally open and spontaneous and feel
like a kid again. It's all about letting the good times roll.

THE MOON

Beware of projections and more projections. If you find yourself feeling unusually paranoid, blame it on the moon. Any
fears or feelings of abandonment that surface are most likely
delusional. But keep your wits about you just in case.

JUDGMENT

Latent feelings may be stirred up. You may be receiving some
sort of wake-up call. Be careful not to be too judgmental
toward yourself or your date.

THE WORLD

Look out—karmic connection ahead. Seeds that were planted
long ago are sprouting, and the roots go very deep. You never
know which past life will be evoked when you pull this card.

Here's the Deal

The most important thing to keep in mind when using tarot for divination is that you are the guide. The cards mirror your thoughts, fears, and hopes. They help you hone your intuition and get in touch with the psychic powers you possess. (Yes, we must remind you, you do have psychic powers.) We recommend studying on your own, meditating on the cards, and practicing on willing friends. And if you can hook up with a talented tarot card reader in your community, you can surely learn a thing or two. Perhaps you'll soon have your own storefront with the requisite crystal ball. We trust that your kerchiefs will be tasteful, and that you'll dispense sage advice to all the confused daters who come to your door.

Section 2

DURING THE DATE

PALMISTRY

A Handy Guide

What kind of date do you have on your hands? Grab
a gander at his appendages and find out who he really is.

The hand is the visible part of the brain.

—GOETHE

HERE AT THE *Fate of Your Date* OFFICES, WE FIRMLY BELIEVE that the humble hand is a supreme source of illuminating information. Our oft-neglected appendages are usually taken for granted, except when we're visiting the manicurist or lost in a daydream about carats and cuts. But let this be a thing of the past. Palmistry is one of the easiest (and most revealing) divinatory arts to master. Not to mention that it's an exceptionally useful tool to keep in your dating divination toolbox. Your hands are a map of your life—past, present, and future. As we grow and transform, our hands tell our stories. The body and mind, intimately interlinked, constantly express themselves on the surface of the skin— most tellingly on the palm. By looking closely at a hand, you can determine the intellect, emotional intensity, and general demeanor of the person attached to it.

The beauty of this divinatory art is that it can be used both pre-date (in the bar or café while you're sizing things up) and on the actual date. By assessing the hands from afar, you can use palmistry to figure out whether the person attached to them merits your attention. And once you get close enough to study the lines on the palm, it's a terrific way to determine whether you've got a worthy specimen at hand (pun intended). In this section we'll give you tips on how to read a hand, and, should you decide that you want to go out with the body and mind attached to it, we'll give you tips on how to undertake a more in-depth palmistry investigation.

A Handy History

Ancient palmistry, the slightly mystical cousin of modern hand analysis, dates back to India at least three thousand years ago. The palmists of yore drew from purely esoteric resources; they didn't know why their methods worked, they just knew that they did. Modern hand analysis is based on a premise similar to that used in acupuncture: our brain functions, nervous systems, and circulatory health can be read on our tongues, faces, and hands. These telltale markings change throughout our lives, depending on wellness, disease, and simple stresses. The brain impulses from our central nervous system travel to our hands, creating a revealing map to read.

Handling the Nuts and Bolts

Luckily, you can use a combination of this ancient art and modern science on your conquest without coming off like Stevie Nicks on a bad hair day. You don't even need to touch the hand in question to elicit the deep (and possibly dirty) secrets hiding in it. Merely observing the size, shape, and color of the hands will tell you volumes about the character and temperament of your subject. Once you've decided to get a little closer, thumb size, hand dominance, and, of course, those myth-laden lines on the palm all come into play.

First and foremost, it's essential to observe the general characteristics of the hand. The basic shape and size can tell us quite a bit about the subject. Is the hand large or small? Long fingered or short? Bony, delicate, or rough-hewn? Do you have chemistry with this pair of hands? Is the grip firm or loose? We don't need to tell you what a limp handshake means. Most important, is this a pair of hands you'd like to hold?

Once you've determined that you like the hands in question, it's time to move on to more in-depth analysis.

BIG HANDS MEAN . . .

✦ ✦ ✦

Big gloves. Ever since Carrie and Samantha debated hand size as a determiner of penis size on Sex and the City, we've been on the case. And while hand size does correlate with certain personality characteristics, our research has revealed that there are plenty of men with small hands and large penises, and vice versa, defying the common myth that large hands mean a large package.

If we could discover an accurate method of divination with regard to this "prickly" issue, we'd be millionaires. According to those trained in hand analysis, large-handed people are inclined to think before they act, while small-handed folks tend to be more spontaneous. You know what they say about big feet, right? That's our next mission.

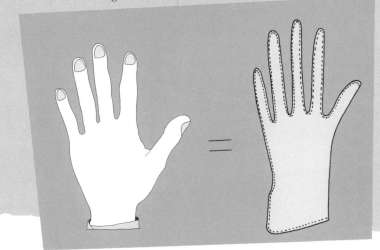

Active versus Passive Hand

First, have you got yourself a lefty or a righty? Handedness is a matter of genetics. About one in ten people are left-handed. If you've got a lefty, expect a left-of-center attitude due to a lifetime of being elbowed, admonished by less-than-understanding teachers, and forced to grapple with tricky soup spoons. If you've found yourself a righty, then you know that this person has had one less painful issue to struggle with (righties were born into society's largest group, so at least they've got that on their side). If your date is ambidextrous, all the more fun for you. The left side of the brain controls the right side of the body, and vice versa. Lefties are thought to be right-brained, and therefore more creative and quirky, since the right side of the brain governs creativity. The left governs logic, so logically, right-handed folks tend to be more logical.

Experts say the less-dominant hand symbolizes the inner self, and the active hand represents the persona. If the markings on the active hand are quite different from those on the passive hand, it indicates that the person has done some serious psychological work and gone through some major changes. You can determine your specimen's dominant hand either by politely asking or by watching which hand is used for writing. Ask for the person's number, or something.

THUMBS UP!

✦ ✦ ✦

The thumb is considered an island unto itself. Its flexibility shows how adaptable a person is. The more flexible the thumb, the more open-minded the individual. A thumb placed high on the hand indicates rigidity, particularly in money matters. (Is this cat paying for dinner, or what?) A low thumb points to generosity and intelligence—a lovely combination, we think. A moderately long thumb indicates intelligence, an ability to execute, and faithfulness. A very long thumb suggests someone who thinks instead of feels—and all head and no heart equals pain. But perhaps you're into that.

  In Touch

So, using the tips outlined above, you've probably done as much analyzing as you can from afar. You've determined the hand's size and shape, the active hand, and the thumb length and position. If you like what you see, you're ready to delve deeper into the art of palm reading. If the date is already getting cozy, dive right in. Apparently you don't need any help from us to get those hot little hands into yours. But if you're looking for a way to get closer, suggest an impromptu palm reading. It's an excellent ploy. You can admit you're reading this book, say that you've been to a palm reader recently, or talk about your gypsy ancestry. It's your call. Either way, you're a sly little dog, aren't you?

Size Matters

If we look at the finger and thumb as appetizers, then the palm is definitely the main course. It shows the deeper levels of the personality and can reflect both recent and long-past experiences. In other words, the palm shows just what kind of lover your date might make.

A narrow palm reveals a lack of imagination. Bor-ing! A wide palm indicates strong health and an even temper, especially when the fingers are proportional to the palm. This is probably a good, sensible catch. An overly wide and thick palm suggests a deceptive individual, prone to exaggeration. Watch out for this one.

NOTE: *Lines on the palm are difficult to see by candlelight, so focus on size and shape if lighting is limited.*

In Living Color

A very pale palm usually indicates selfishness. If you're hearing too much "I, me, mine," it's likely your date possesses a narrow palm and we say it's fair to fake an emergency to

escape the date. A yellowish palm shows a morbid and bilious disposition; if your date's not laughing at all your genius jokes, now you know why. A pink and mottled palm indicates a hopeful disposition. A reddish palm might mean a quick temper, so test the waters before you go on a second date.

The Mounts

Sorry, but the mounts don't *necessarily* have anything to do with sex (except in certain cases, which we'll discuss in a moment). Instead, the mounts are merely positions on the palm associated with the celestial bodies. You'll find seven mounts on the hand, but for our purposes the most important one is the Mount of Venus, which symbolizes love, romance, and affection. It sits beneath the base of the thumb and above the wrist (see point A). A very pronounced Mount of Venus indicates a Venusian type, the very best kind (at least in our opinion). A springy, fleshy Mount of Venus shows a strong libido. A flabby one, with loose skin, indicates a lower sex drive. Lots of horizontal lines on the Mount of Venus indicate well-developed charms, and usually a history of sexual conquests. (Don't say we didn't warn you.) An intricate pattern of vertical and horizontal lines here shows a compli-cated romantic life, and possibly some

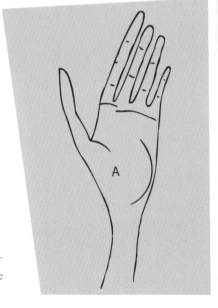

unresolved past pain. The other mounts correspond to Jupiter, Saturn, Apollo, Mercury, Mars, and the moon. The most prominent mount on the hand and its corresponding planet suggests the dominant characteristics of the individual. Refer to the astrology books listed on page 159 for more information on planets and their meanings.

The Lines

Here's where we get to down to the nitty-gritty. We're going to look at the three major lines on a palm—the heart line, the head line, and the life line. Always start with the more prominent hand.

HEART LINE

The heart line indicates the romantic temperament, so check it first and pay close attention. The higher it sits on the hand, the more passionate (and sometimes jealous) a person may be. If the heart line lies straight across the palm, it points to a certain stinginess (read: emotional tightwads). Keep this in mind if your greatest fear is spending your next relationship asking, "Honey, what are you thinking about?" A line that sharply curves under the first or second finger shows a lovey-dovey, super-romantic person—a sweep-you-off-your-feet type. (Caveat: These sorts tend to fall in and out of love fast. We like to call this one the "player heart line.") A straight heart line suggests someone less demonstrative, but also more reliable. A forked heart line shows someone who's got a little bit of both.

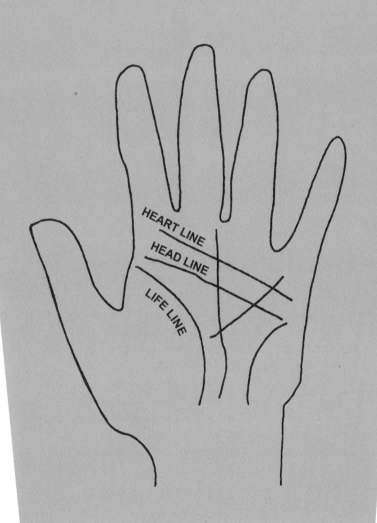

HEART LINE

HEAD LINE

LIFE LINE

LIFE LINE

The life line, which represents vitality and life force, runs downward, curving around the base of the thumb. A short life line does not indicate imminent death. It might suggest, rather, pessimism, dullness, and shortsightedness. A long life line is seen in people who know exactly what they want out of life.

HEAD LINE

The head line is the middle horizontal line on the palm and it tells you the sort of intellect you're dealing with. If you're all for a date who dazzles you with witty bon mots, look here first. A straight, unbroken line may be seen in someone whose thinking style is practical and cautious. A curved head line reveals a creative type, while a wavy head line shows indecisiveness.

Wrapped Around Your Finger

Now that you have the goods on palmistry, stop your hand wringing and start analyzing all the hands you come into contact with, starting with your very own. Practice makes perfect, and it brings you one step closer to getting your date into the palm of your hand.

FACE TIME

The Art of Face Reading and Body Language Basics

Face it: you're dying to know what those expressions really mean. Get behind the mask with the art of face reading.

WE ALL PUT ON A GOOD FACE DURING FIRST DATES, talk up our best qualities, and rehearse the perfect answer to every possible personal question. Perhaps we don't lie intentionally, but we don't come out and announce any of the following: "It took an hour to blow my hair to make it look this natural," "I got a zit the size of Mount Vesuvius before my last period," "I'm a little bit, well, *nutty* without my meds." We assume that if a relationship develops, all of our not-ready-for-prime-time behavior will come out eventually, and our date can decide whether to pursue us, preferably after they're already safely whipped. We keep it nice in the beginning, because we simply want to make a fabulous impression. Unless we're on a blind date that we want to ditch, we generally put our best face forward.

And apparently, so do our dates, those slippery little worms. They've studied the same book of tricks that we have, and they know how to conceal their less attractive behavior, at least verbally. Ex-cons don't go around advertising their former cell numbers (no, we don't mean their mobile phones), and guys with raging mother complexes do their best to keep their skeletons safely ensconced in the closet (usually at least until after you fall for them). Lucky for you, this chapter offers countless tips on how to read body language and facial expressions, so you can know what you're getting into.

The face and body offer a veritable gold mine of information about your date's true self. The art of face reading originated in ancient Greece and China as a divinatory tool. Aristotle is credited with writing a lengthy treatise on face reading, and the Greeks even used face reading theories to create the masks they wore for theatrical performances. In China, face reading began in the first century B.C. as an adjunct to Confucianism. For the Chinese, face reading took on more of a medical bent used to analyze physical health and vitality. Present-day professional face readers take their cue, in part, from ancient traditions, but they have thrown a whole lot of science into the mix. Modern medicine and empirical data have given face reading some serious street cred—it's now used by psychologists, criminologists, and antiterrorist bounty hunters. After taking our tour of contemporary face reading, you'll soon be a walking poly-graph, able to detect common dating lies in a single bound (or glance).

Facing It

We may not know it, but we're basically hardwired to read each other's faces. We can detect a friendly smile from 150 feet away. Darwin figured it out a long time ago: Understanding expressions is a key to human survival. When that giant, hungry saber-toothed tiger was about to descend on the clan, the facial expression that said, "Scared Shitless: Run!" was invaluable before our ancestors had the proper language for such warnings. We're an interdependent and social species, and our faces tell our stories.

In Your Face

Faces can be studied in various ways. One can analyze the shape of the face and the features in order to glean clues about the personality, history, and potential of anyone not wearing a ski mask. There are three levels of analysis: First, you can interpret unchanging features like the size and shape of the face, shape and placement of features, and so on. (We focus here on the eyes.) Second, you can analyze gradual changes to the face, including wrinkles and lines. (Since the arrival of Botox, this is a bit less reliable, but it still works for the most part.) Third, you can examine expression, movement, and general body language. We suggest that you start at the beginning. Our overview blends ancient Chinese, Greek, and modern theories of this art-science.

GRIN AND BARE IT

✦ ✦ ✦

From whence did the smile evolve? Its origins may not be as innocent as you would expect. Many anthropologists believe that smiles evolved from the baring of teeth, which cavemen used to try to entice caveladies into sleeping with them. When they found that sort of fierce wooing to be ineffective, they learned to mask their beastly desire and disarm innocent lasses with their "smiles." Men never change.

Private Eyes Are Watching You

Much more than mere windows to the soul, the eyes are exemplary communicators of deception, stress, and sadness.

The size of the iris indicates the nature of one's childhood. A negative environment as a child causes a smaller iris, which may indicate an extremely sensitive person who needs a lot of reassurance. A large, full iris points to an emotional openness and a love of communication.

When the whites of the eyes are visible beneath the iris and above the lower lid, it indicates a heightened degree of mental stress and worry. If you spot more white showing in the left eye, this means the stress is likely caused by personal issues. If you see more white showing in the right eye, it usually indicates business or financial issues. When the whites of the eyes show above the iris, the degree of stress is so high that violence is possible, so watch your ass— your subject is probably in fight-or-flight mode. If the whites of the eyes show *all the way* around the iris, beware, because this likely means that there is some sort of extreme mental disconnect going on. This is serious stuff—like shock or an acid trip.

Thick eyelashes indicate a tolerant, gentle disposition, while thin lashes suggest excessive sensitivity and a quick temper. (Mascara can be deceptive, though.)

Puffy eyelids suggest more than just a hard night of drinking or a work-oriented all-nighter. According to face-reading theorists, eyelids that are always moderately puffy suggest

HEADS UP

✦ ✦ ✦

Phrenology, a charmingly hokey pseudoscience, was the brainchild of a nineteenth-century Viennese doctor named Franz Joseph Gall. It employs a scalp massage of sorts for gaining insight into the specimen's personality by feeling the contours of the skull. It was also a repulsive post-Enlightenment excuse for all sorts of racism. We won't even go there. After a run of popular acceptance in the United States, it was eventually refuted and relegated to the annals of history as the joke that it is.

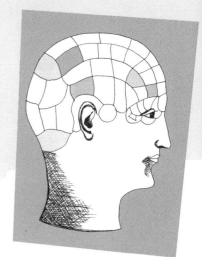

an impatient and critical person—one not prone to having a very good time. Tell your puffy-lidded friend to start having fun, posthaste. If the left eyelid seems puffier, the personal life is in tumult, and if the right eyelid looks puffier, your subject's business or professional life is taking a beating.

If the skin over the eyelids hangs down over the eye in a serious way, it indicates defensiveness, selfishness, self-denial, and a desperate need for a more positive outlook.

If your date can't look you in the eyes, you may have a problem. Sometimes this can indicate mere shyness, so give it a little time. If your subject doesn't get comfortable after about twenty minutes of chatting, you may be dealing with someone so painfully shy or so socially inept that the date may be more work than pleasure. However, the inability to look a person in the eye can also point to shiftiness. Gently keep trying to make eye contact and see what happens. On the other hand, if your date barely knows you, but stares into your limpid pools relentlessly, without blinking, this person may be a bit unbalanced.

LYING EYES

✦ ✦ ✦

When a person tells a bald-faced lie, the pupils dilate for a split second. It takes a while to learn to detect this nuance, but you can play truth-or-dare with friends and test out the theory for yourself. Ask them to make five statements: three false, and two true. Observe their pupils and take notes. Then have them 'fess up regarding each statement. Eventually you'll get the hang of it.

The Lineup

Just like the lines on a palm, facial markings are intimate and intricate maps of our personal histories and psychic wounds. Careful observation of facial lines and wrinkles can tell you more about your date in a few minutes than a lifetime of repeating "Honey, why don't you let me in?" Meanwhile, society has created a multibillion-dollar industry dedicated to the eradication of wrinkles and lines. From microderm-abrasion to $150 jars of "miracle cream," we are obsessed with making our lines invisible. Maybe that's because they reveal so much of who we really are.

When looking at your subject's face, remember these lessons for reading facial lines:

1. The deeper the line, the deeper the issue, and

2. the lines on the left side of the face correspond to the inner world, while markings on the right side of the face correspond to the outer world.

Horizontal lines on the forehead point to well-developed mental abilities. Three or more of them suggest that the person has worked very hard on something either in a short period of time or across a lifetime. These lines can also indi-cate genius in one's chosen field. Several broken lines indicate multiple mental interests.

Diagonal lines on the forehead suggest some stringent mental pressure in the past, or some mental discipline imposed from outside sources. Recent grads and overachievers in general tend to sport these lines.

A single deep vertical line between the eyebrows indicates extreme self-discipline and/or self-sacrifice.

Two vertical lines between the eyebrows suggest that this person is too self-critical.

Many lines between the eyebrows mean that the subject is a perfectionist.

Three lines forming a triangle between the eyebrows are called "visionary lines" and may express a strong inner wisdom.

Many fine lines at the top of the bridge of the nose suggest a hyper-responsible person who usually takes on too much.

The "burnout" line carves itself deeply at the top of the bridge of the nose. This line suggests someone who's taken on so much that a breakdown is approaching. Send that person to a spa, pronto.

Lines that radiate from the outside corners of the eyes, otherwise known as "crow's feet," are thought of as "big picture" lines. They suggest wisdom or lack of gullibility, which may be derived from the concept of "the wisdom of the crow."

Let's Get Physical

After you've given the face a once-over, take a close look
at what your date's body is doing. An astute observation
of body language can reveal much more than the conversation.
Face and body-language reading are widely used in jury
selection and sales training — they're not just for sizing up
your date. Observe, and ye shall learn perhaps too much.

THE HANDS HAVE IT

If your date seems to want to hide one hand in a pocket
or under the table, note which hand it is. Hiding the left
hand suggests that the person has secrets of the emotional,
intimate variety and wants to conceal information about past
relationships or emotional difficulties. A hidden right hand
can mean secrets of a less personal nature; say, embezzlement
or grand larceny.

Upturned palms can indicate deception.

People who steeple their hands (see illustration) want to be
in control, or at least appear in control.

Covering the thumbs with the other fingers can mean that
this person feels anxious and threatened.

If your date makes gestures with a stiff or pointed thumb
or a rigid hand in general, it suggests a desire to dominate

you somehow. This person will be unlikely to budge when you have a disagreement.

Scratching or rubbing the top of the head suggests more than a need for some dandruff sham-poo. It can mean that your date is a little bit confused and mentally blocked.

Rubbing the brow suggests doubt or worry.

Tapping the space between the eyebrows is a signal that your date is searching for an answer or trying to remember something.

Rubbing the eyes suggests a state of mental exhaustion or feeling overburdened.

People who touch their nose are feeling pressured or con-trolled by something. Or they might be allergic to you, of course. But if this gesture is combined with many trips to the WC, we have another problem altogether.

Fingertips touching the temple suggest that your date may have had enough of your jabbering and is quickly approaching the mental saturation point.

If your date covers their mouth while listening to you it means that a critical evaluation is in progress, or that this skeptic doesn't believe a word you're saying.

On the other hand, dates who cover their mouths while *they're* talking may be hiding something, or feeling particularly shy.

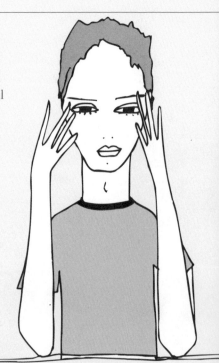

Holding the chin represents an unconscious desire for more power. The chin is the personal symbol of power and aggressiveness.

If your date pulls at the skin of the throat, there may be some issues with self-expression.

People who pull on their lips are thought to be overly greedy.

Pulling on the jowl expresses fear about one's sexual desirability. They may think you're just not that into them. If you are, this is a good time to put your hand on the person's knee. Everybody knows what *that* means.

Rubbing behind the ears signifies a fear of being misunderstood.

Rubbing on the back of the neck says, "I'd rather not deal with that right now, thank you."

Arms folded across the chest suggest self-protection or holding firm to a position.

Drooping shoulders indicate weight-of-the-world syndrome — this person may feel overwhelmed by life.

Arms kept behind the back suggest a fear of intimacy.

Bouncing legs and tapping fingers on the table spell anxiety.

Leaning away says, "I want to get out of here as quickly as possible."

Leaning forward suggests attentiveness and interest.

MONA LISA SMILE

✦ ✦ ✦

The act of smiling bathes our brains in a shower of addictive neurotransmitters. However, when you have to smile for a picture, or you smile at someone you don't really like, you don't get that same joyful hormone brain bath. Authentic smiles engage the eyes and are called "felt" smiles. We hope you smile this way when you first meet your date. It's a smile of connection, of fate, of having met your life partner. Or maybe it's just a smile that says, "I'm going to get laid! Yahoo!"

Body of Evidence

It's a lot to take in, we know. Put all of this dating data to the test in small doses. You don't want to be so pre-occupied analyzing body language that you don't hear a word he's saying. Witty repartee is still worth something.

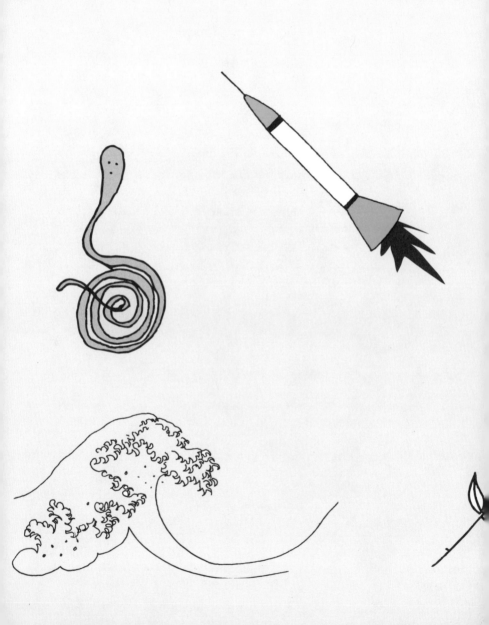

YOU'RE NOT GETTING ANY JUNGER

Interpreting Symbols during a Date

Sign up for a lesson in symbolism: learn what those moments really mean.

Trust that which gives you meaning and accept it as your guide.
——CARL JUNG

Symbols are everywhere. We live, breathe, and devour the symbols of our universe every single moment of our lives. Missiles are not shaped that way by accident, for example. Men have been building things in their own images for a while now. Georgia O'Keeffe painted exquisite flowers to symbolize, well, you know. Symbols are sometimes intentional and sometimes unconscious. But we digress.

This Is Your Brain; This Is Your Brain on Jung

First came Freud, and then came Jung, his mystical disciple. Rather than obsessing on sex and death, as his predecessor did, Carl Jung fell in love with the world of myth and symbol. His profound little theory was that all human beings from time immemorial are connected by a series of images and ideas called archetypes. These symbols reach across cultures and millennia, and rarely do they vary. For instance, water is the universal symbol for the subconscious. Snakes are widely and famously thought of as symbols of the phallus and the trickster. All of human history, embedded in our DNA, contributes to our dreams, our unconscious thoughts, our everything—known as the "collective unconscious." Imagine it as a giant, cosmic mainframe computer. We're all connected to it with our psychic Wi-Fi cards.

If we accept this theory (which we do, by the way) then we open ourselves up to so much wonderful serendipity. Since we're all connected, we can send each other psychic messages. We're constantly exchanging files—call them "energy mails." In addition, the universe sends us messages. We just need to be open to sending and receiving all this correspondence. The other theory we hope you accept is that time is not linear. It's all sort of happening at the same time— all in the soup at once, if you will. (Einstein thought so too, and he expressed it in his fancy theory of relativity.)

OK, OK, enough jabber. What does this mean for *you*? It simply means that you should keep all of your senses attuned to the myriad symbols that are likely to appear to you during your date.

Although many symbols or archetypes are universal, none of this stuff is written in stone. It's all very, very open to your interpretation, and that of your girlfriends over a round of apple martinis. This chapter aims to get you thinking about life (and your date) unfolding in a symbolic way. Learning to hone your intuition will help in this endeavor.

Sign Language

You can start to observe symbols even before you know exactly what you're looking for. In the beginning, just keep an open mind. Once you've attuned yourself to the very idea of symbols appearing in your field of vision, you'll begin to pick up signs everywhere—mostly when you're not even looking for them.

The following is a starter list that you'll surely add to as your intuition broadens.

THE INITIAL MEETING

What was the weather like when you met? Gloomy, stormy, or sunny and bright? Or was a thunderstorm raging, perhaps?

Did any animals cross your path that day? Were they cute and cuddly critters, or were they snakes or cockroaches?

Birds are thought to symbolize human souls—they can indicate new relationships with a lot of open communication, since they relate to the air element. (One of your humble authors was shat upon by a pigeon, *directly on her third eye*, moments after leaving a date. Needless to say, he turned out to be very, very bad for her.)

What was the name of the store, bar, restaurant, or street corner where you first met?

Who were you with when you first met your date? The backstabbing lunatic from your office, or your best girlfriend whom you love like a sister?

What was your mood or state of health right before you met? If you woke up with the sniffles or food poisoning on the day of the date, consider what the universe might be telling you.

Did you meet on or near an important date for you, such as a birthday or anniversary?

ON THE DATE
Watch for the appearance of symbols on the big day, starting from the moment you wake up.

What is the day's major headline? If all seems right with the world, you may have a happy-ever-after situation on your hands. If there's more war and strife than ever, look out.

What song is playing in the car, bar, or restaurant? One of your faves, maybe a love song? Your song with your last, awful boyfriend who broke your heart?

What's the waiter's energy like? Watch out for spills and broken plates. If the waitstaff are super nice and you're all vibing happily, good energy is surely bouncing around and this can bode well. Or maybe you should just go home with the waiter.

What are the people sitting next to you talking about? Are they cooing or fighting? Take note.

What color is your date wearing? Whites and other light colors symbolize innocence and a childlike outlook. Just like with roses, red is seductive, yellow is friendly, and blue will soothe you.

Anything written on your date's T-shirt? Heed all messages.

If your date has a hat on, it might represent an attempt to repress something inside the person's head. Unless it's just cold out.

Who was the last person to call you before your date? Was it a good, bad, or neutral phone call? If it was your boss calling to scream at you, it could be a bad omen.

If your cell rings in the middle of the date, who's calling and for what? (This doesn't include any friend you've enlisted to make an emergency get-me-out-of-this-freaking-date call.) Is it your most needy friend, your most annoying friend, your truest friend, or your craziest friend?

Anything you see, feel, hear, smell, or touch on your date can be interpreted as a sign. Signs might be warning you away from a relationship by reminding you of some negative past association. If you believe in the concept of karma, this is just a way to prevent you from accumulating any new bad juju. Maybe you met your date in a past life, had a failed marriage, and spent the rest of that life with a broken heart. Maybe you broke your date's heart two thousand years ago and if you got together again you'd surely get yours trampled. Positive signs, on the other hand, can indicate that you're really meant to be with this person. If you wake up feeling great on the morning of your date, you hit every green light on the way to work, your cappuccino has the perfect froth, and the news says that world peace is not far away, you might be in for a delightful date come evening—and possibly a winning new relationship.

This is precisely why we should open our hearts and minds to symbols, rather than relying purely on attraction and witty repartee. Pay attention to every sign on the road, because they can save you lots of grief later on.

We often ignore symbols because we find them implausible or inconvenient. But they really are nature's warning signals, doing their best to light your way. Heed them, please.

Section 3

AFTER THE DATE

BEWITCHED, BOTHERED, AND BEWILDERED

Spell Craft

Witch way do you turn for the perfect date? Learn how
to put a spell on him.

YOU'VE ALWAYS BEEN A LITTLE BIT CRAFTY. But in a good way, of course. After all, how else could you get by in this crazy, painful world? In life and love, a little bit of craftiness is nothing to feel guilty about. Spell craft is the pièce de résistance of the divination universe. With a few carefully crafted spells, you can proactively put to use all the mysterious energies we've been telling you about. The art of casting spells, or, as we like to call it, white magic, is all about focusing on your desires, drawing the world's energy together, and setting it loose to make your dreams come true. It's one of the most powerful of the divinatory arts.

You may be surprised at how widely white magic is used today. While it is indeed an ancient practice with a rich history, it's still practiced in parts of Africa, as well as by Native Americans and by the Creoles of Haiti (they're the ones who do voodoo). And today, thousands of women and men around the world practice Wicca, a modern form of white magic that is totally egalitarian and Birkenstock friendly. Like several of the other divinatory arts in this book, Wicca reemerged in full force during the twentieth century, particularly in the last thirty years.

Perhaps the reason why it's so popular is because it makes the world a better place. Its very premise is "Do no harm."

That's the first thing that little witches learn. Every time you cast a spell, the spell must spell good in the world. And what spells *good* better than l-o-v-e?

But before we get into the wonders of white magic and how to harness its powers, we should touch on its evil twin, black magic. Unlike white magic, black magic uses the darker forces of energy in the universe. It's very, very dangerous. Now, we understand that working a little black magic may seem like a good idea if you find yourself snubbed or wronged. But be warned—you should never, ever use magic to harm. Ever. Even if he's broken your heart and you want to rip his out, the consequences of using magic for unsavory purposes are very, very bad. You see, the principle of karma plays a big role in witchy activities. What goes around comes around—perhaps not in the form that you might expect, but it does indeed come around.

 That Voodoo That You Do

OK, so you've set your sights on a cutie pie. You've decided that this is the one you want. Now it's time to make it so. As we said above, white magic is pretty potent stuff. It's not something to be taken lightly. Even if you've taken the "do no harm" oath, you're dealing with delicate yet powerful

energetic forces. So be careful. However, we have to stress that while white magic is powerful, it can't change what isn't meant to be. If he's not into you, you can't use white magic to make him like you. Sorry, ladies. But if he *is* into you and just doesn't know it yet, you can speed up the process. If he's shy, you can help to draw him out of his shell. If he's not sexed up enough for your taste, you can turn on the cosmic Viagra. If he's lying, you can find out, and then dump him promptly. Further down the line, if he's thinking about asking you to marry him, you can use white magic to seal the deal. White magic may not be the great equalizer, but it can be the great accelerator, used in the right way. Keep in mind that the most important element of white magic is creative visualization. If you can visualize what you want, you'll find it easier to gather the energy together to make it happen. Some of us excel at the art of visualization. The rest of us may be a little challenged. If you're not in the God-given-talent club, prepare to practice a bit.

Let it be understood that an authentic study of white magic is a complex and many-splendored thing. We've provided a few spells below for some pretty standard dating situations. But if you're looking for more in-depth information, you can easily find a *ton* of fantastic books on the topic. We've listed a few on page 159. White magic is a spiritual discipline, one that's as valid as any you may have been born into, but it's also extremely accessible and modern, and it's got some compelling pop cachet. It takes years to earn your broomstick, and it cannot be rushed. However, the simple spells following just might improve your dating life markedly. Who knows—you may start your very own coven one day.

She's Crafty

Every spell session calls for a state of deep introspection and meditation, or at least as much as you can manage in the midst of extreme dating anxiety. Try to breathe, breathe, and breathe some more. Find yourself a quiet room. Turn off the phone, the computer, and the TV. Then let the magic begin.

SPELL SCHEDULING

✦ ✦ ✦

Spells can be done any day of the week, but love spells work best on 1) Fridays (the day of Venus); 2) when the moon is in Libra or Taurus (both ruled by Venus); and 3) during a waxing moon in the sign of the potential lover in question. Scorpio moons are great for sex spells, FYI. You can always cast a spell when you feel the need, but the universe will throw you an extra bone if you plan in accordance with the planets.

ALTARS

+ + +

Witches really dig their altars. But these setups don't need to be chock-a-block with tchotchkes and knickknacks. Altars are simply sacred spaces created for practicing rituals. In white magic, outdoor spaces are often used. But if you're stuck inside, just find a table, desk, or other area where you feel comfortable working magic. It's lovely to sit in front of an open window where you can see the moon and the stars, and tune into their energy.

If you want to create your own semi-permanent mini-altar, there are dozens of ways to personalize it. You can use it to store common ritual tools, such as candles, matches, notebooks for recording spells (also called the "Book of Shadows"), or any object that has meaning for you. You may want to keep a vase full of fresh flowers as an offering to the higher spirit of your choice.

The following spells have been taken from a veritable witch's brew of brilliant books and adapted for your dating pleasure. Feel free to personalize them further; it's not about the tools—it's about the intention.

THE CLARITY SPELL (OR "SHIT OR GET OFF THE POT ALREADY, DOOFUS!")

If your intended is wishy-washy (possibly a Libra or Gemini) and you can't nail down a vibe no matter what you do, this spell will help clear the air.

YOU'LL NEED

+ A glass of clear liquid (water, Sprite, white wine—whatever floats your boat, baby)
+ A piece of blank paper
+ A red pen

Sit down at a table (or your altar) with all your tools and get comfy. Take three deep breaths, focus, and visualize your intended. Write down exactly what you would say to your

date if you had the cojones: "Why are you torturing me? Are you really attracted to women, or what? You're destroying my self-esteem, you mofo." Whatever you need to say or ask, write it on the paper. As you continue to focus on finding the truth, drink down the liquid. (If you're drinking alcohol, this is not an excuse to pound it.) Place the glass on the table. Then repeat the following three times: "I drink from the water of clarity to get a final answer. Within forty-eight hours I will know how you feel. So mote it be." (*Mote* is fun witch language for "Goddess, make this happen!")

Get ready for some defining event to occur. If you wake up to the typical "I just got booked for an eight-week business trip to Thailand" e-mail, you'll know exactly what it means. Or perhaps you'll meet someone else, or you'll decide that the thrill is gone, or a fresh bouquet of roses will arrive at your door. Somehow, the answer will appear. Who needs *He's Just Not That into You* when you've got a spell that helps you get the answers you need?

THE ALWAYS-POPULAR "TOUCH ME, YOU FOOL!" SPELL

This is a straight-up seduction spell. If your would-be lover is hanging around, asking you out on still more dates, and acting all nervous and weird, but hasn't kissed you yet, this spell will hit the ball out of the park. You can decide on the bases later on. This spell works wonderfully well under a Scorpio moon and it's more effective if done between eleven and midnight.

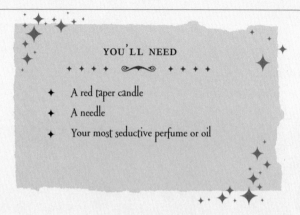

YOU'LL NEED

+ + + + ❧ + + + +

+ A red taper candle
+ A needle
+ Your most seductive perfume or oil

Go to your altar or other quiet space and get into meditation mode. Take three deep breaths. With the needle, write on the side of the candle both your initials and the initials of the crazy-making fool who won't touch you. Then place it firmly in a safe candleholder, away from drapes and pesky cats. You'll be burning this one down to the base, so make sure it's well protected. Next, anoint the candle by rubbing a few drops of your perfume over the engraved initials. (No, we don't recommend that you pour out your entire $250 bottle of Chanel No. 5 for this project. Go easy.) As you sensually rub your candle (hint, hint—we know what you're thinking and we like it), imagine your soon-to-be lover caressing and kissing you. Do this for as long as it feels right. Pierce the candle crosswise with the needle, right through the center. Then light it and repeat this mantra three times: "By the time this candle burns down, (insert name) will burn for me. So mote it be." Now go get waxed, because you're gonna get some real soon.

THE "GET THAT BASTARD OUT OF MY HEAD" LETTING-GO SPELL

You were brave enough to dive in headfirst. You lived, you loved, and that asshole broke your fragile heart. Curse him! Actually, don't curse him, because the karma will come back to haunt you. Instead, cleanse your soul with a spell and move on to greater and greener dating pastures. This spell is good anytime but will work best during a last-quarter moon.

YOU'LL NEED

✦ Flowers or flower essence
(use pansies or violets, if available)

Draw yourself a hot bath. Fill the tub with flowers. Climb in and begin to meditate on all the reasons you need to let go of this past, destructive love. If you weren't loved well enough, promise yourself that you'll only pursue those who can love you as much as you deserve. If you were lied to, focus on attracting only honest partners in the future. If no one was at fault but it just didn't work out, ask the universe to lead you in the right direction. When you're all shriveled up and properly hypnotized by the witchy energies you've conjured,

drain the tub. As you watch the water swirl down, imagine all those negative emotions getting sucked into the center of the earth, or into the local sewage station. Utter this mantra: "I will leave the past in the past, and move on to an even better future. So mote it be." Repeat this until all the water has been drained. Do this ritual as many times as you need to over the course of a two-week healing period. And if you get a booty call from the heartbreaker, you know what to do. (We suggest deleting all offending numbers from your cell phone and blocking e-mails and instant messages from the creep.)

Spelling It Out

The essence of spell craft is intention. You can build worlds with the power of your mind. You can harness energy to make it real. But in order for white magic to work, you have to believe that thoughts are actually things. You have to believe in the power of your mind, the weight of your emotions, and the interconnection of all things on earth. Spells are fun, but the underlying white magic is serious stuff. Witches have been persecuted for thousands of years because, when it comes down to it, they're actually the most powerful people on the planet. And remember, as we've mentioned before, every lady has a little witch in her wardrobe.

DREAM A
LITTLE DREAM

Astral Travel and Dream Analysis

Wake up to the ways in which your dreams can improve your dating life.

IF YOU'RE LOOKING FOR A DREAM DATE, look no further than your dreams. Tapping into the power of dreams can greatly improve your dating life and your waking life overall. Dreams hold a vast store of deep and entrenched unconscious impulses and information about your life—past, present, and future. And your dreams are *your* dreams, your personal, private resource to tap at your will.

We spend a third of our lives asleep, and 15 to 25 percent of that time is devoted to dreaming. Dreams provide a sanctuary from the hustle and bustle of our workaday world. When awakening from a great fantasy dream, we long to reenter the cave of the dream and stay there. Where else do we get to finally kiss our secret crush, stroll a beautiful beach in the dead of winter, or even fly? On the flip side, we are often startled by disturbing dreams, and their residue can stick with us for days. That bad date from a few months back might continue to crop up again and again, long after you've blocked the jerk's e-mail address. Science has not yet developed a mind filter to keep spam-laden dates out of our dreams.

It's important to note that *everyone* dreams, although some of us have better recall than others. There are those who claim that they don't dream at all. But those people are wrong. If you're one of them, we'd like to challenge you to a dream duel. You *do* dream, and you can become a master of your dream world and, consequently, of your dating world. It just takes a little practice.

Some cultures believe that the dream state is an alternate reality and that the experiences we have in our dreams are just as valid as those in our waking lives. Freud and Jung would agree that dream experiences have as much impact on our psyches as waking ones do. They theorized that dreams act as venues for our deepest unconscious workouts, places where we deal with the things that we just can't touch while awake. Freud claimed that we deal with our buried sexual impulses in dreams, and Jung believed that dreams have a spiritual purpose. Both would disagree with scientists who believe that dreaming is simply a biochemical impulse, merely a way to process and discard the detritus of the day. For the record, we too disagree.

Going Astral

If we put some stock in the concept of alternate dimensions and recognize that the physical reality we experience is merely

the tip of the iceberg (your local quantum physicist can help you with this), it's easy to take a leap into the realm of the astral. Put aside the fact that some pretty freaky people espoused the benefits of astral projection in the 1970s. We prefer heels and martinis to loose white robes and bean sprouts, but we're firmly enough entrenched in this dimension to believe that other dimensions do indeed exist. The astral dimension is simply the place that your spiritual body goes when you sleep. Once your physical body relaxes into the sleep state, your spiritual body is freer to travel. The super-cool thing about the astral dimension is that you can meet up and hang out with other astral bodies there. This is a great way to heal broken relationships without stooping to the indignity of drunk dialing or the other ego-bruising activities that we sometimes choose in the desperation of waking life.

 Dreamweaver

Because the astral realm is not confined to the rules of physics as we experience them in daily life, we can instantly hook up with anyone we need to see. Forget waiting for the phone to ring in the astral realm. If a paramour seems to be blowing you off, you can insist on an explanation in your dream, and then wake up satisfied. It takes some training to get there, but we have faith in you.

149

Intention is everything when it comes to mastering the astral realm. Short of projecting yourself into the actual bedroom of someone you're lusting after, you can simply direct your unconscious toward certain experiences while sleeping. For example, while lying in bed, think deeply about the person you want to encounter in your dreams. You're automatically connected to a web of spiritual energy once you fall asleep. The trick is to retain the wisdom by remembering the dream when you wake up. It also helps to keep in mind that the other spiritual bodies you want to encounter also need to be open to dealing with *you*. When you first start an astral experiment, you probably won't know the difference between dream images constructed purely by your psyche and actual encounters with spiritual bodies. But with enough practice (and study) you'll be able to tell the difference. And it doesn't matter much at first, because you'll get the same sort of closure from either kind of experience. Even if it's just your own psyche sending you down the appropriate path, it's all good.

If you'd like to arrange an astral meeting with your intended tonight, however, we must warn you to be patient. The art of astral travel takes practice. Start dream dialing slowly, and eventually you'll tap into that unconscious Palm Pilot with ease. When you get there, you'll be able to ask direct questions and get the answers you seek. If you've received an ambiguous blow-off and you want to know what's up, you can find out astrally. Whether you're the dumper or the dumpee, you can resolve issues in the astral realm that in real life might be awkward or impossible to address.

Lucid Dreaming

Lucid dreaming is the holy grail of the dream universe.
Becoming an expert makes you literally the master of your
dreams. A lucid dream is simply a dream in which you know
that you are dreaming. Once you become aware of your
dream state, you can direct the dream any which way you
want. Want to learn to fly so you can spy on your date
without having to drive across town and hide in the bushes?
Go for it. Want to kick the ass of the date who did you

wrong? No problem. Want to see what's behind curtain number three? Easy as pie. Want to ravage the cutie from the coffee shop who's been ignoring you for the last three months? Want to ask Albert Einstein a question? No worries. It's all yours. When you are lucid in a dream, you can do anything you want, and you're completely in control.

Sometimes lucid dreaming happens spontaneously. Usually it lasts for just a few moments and then it's gone. But you can train to become an expert lucid dreamer, and do it every night if you want to.

The basic tenets of learning to dream lucidly are the same as those for basic dream recall (see "Total Recall," below)

TOTAL RECALL

✦ ✦ ✦

Admit it. You know that Pavlov was right; you're just a dog waiting for a treat. The good news on this front is that our minds are as easily trained as a pooch's. We lose what we don't use, and this applies to dreaming. The simple act of placing a pen and pad of paper by your bedside table will encourage your lazy mind to retain information. Then, the moment you wake up, quickly record whatever you remember. The filter of waking reality kills the dream images quickly. Even if you're awash in grog, start scribbling. You'll get better at this with practice. If you can remember to dab perfume behind your ear before a date, you can remember your dreams.

and astral experimentation: intention is everything. Before bed, repeat a lucid dreaming mantra, such as "Tonight I will awaken in my dreams and take control." Keep that pad and pen at your bedside as encouragement. Dedicate yourself to a regular practice and don't slack. It may not happen right away, but you have to keep trying. Practice is extremely rewarding.

This is a sophisticated practice that has been the subject of many books and experiments, and has made many dreamers happy. If you're interested, we suggest that you study up, because lucid dreaming can open a whole new world. (See page 159 for books on lucid dreaming.)

To Sleep, Perchance to Dream

To encourage you further in your dream travels, here are some hints to become a better dreamer:

Slip a sprig of rosemary under your pillow to help you recall your dreams.

Just saying "I will remember my dreams tonight" out loud is a great way to train the mind for better dream recall. Record dreams immediately upon waking. Don't worry about punctuation or even making sense—just get down as many images and as much information as you can.

A mini-dictaphone placed at the bedside is a great alternative to paper and pen, especially for those who write like doctors.

Don't consume stimulants or depressants near bedtime —
avoid chocolate, caffeinated tea, coffee, and alcohol after six
in the evening, if you can.

Some suggest waking slowly and gently, without an alarm.
If you do need to use an alarm, and you wake up at the same
time every day, you can set the alarm to go off ten minutes
earlier than your usual time. This can cut into your REM
sleep and help you to remember your dreams.

 ## Dream Within a Dream

There is major crossover inherent in dreaming — you are both
in the astral realm and awash in your own private unconscious universe. Everything seems to be connected. You're
working out your father issues and dealing with memories
from your tenth birthday party, while mingling with the
energies of your whole karmic family. The landscape might
look like a Dalí painting. There's your date from last week,
dressed in a clown suit. What does it mean? Only you (and
possibly your therapist) know. No one's been able to figure
out the exact boundaries of this strange and fascinating
universe quite yet. Perhaps you'll be the first to do so, and
in the process make your dating life dreamier than you
ever imagined.

CONCLUSION

Go Forth into the Divine

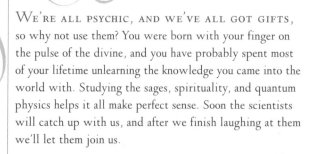

WE'RE ALL PSYCHIC, AND WE'VE ALL GOT GIFTS, so why not use them? You were born with your finger on the pulse of the divine, and you have probably spent most of your lifetime unlearning the knowledge you came into the world with. Studying the sages, spirituality, and quantum physics helps it all make perfect sense. Soon the scientists will catch up with us, and after we finish laughing at them we'll let them join us.

It is your divine right to arm yourself with all of the information contained in this book. This esoteric knowledge shall no longer be relegated to the domain of specialists. You are special, dear reader. To us, in fact, you are *the* specialist.

Our aim has been to demystify divination. We hope that you are thoroughly demystified, clued in, and prepared to continue honing your precious gifts. If you don't use them, you'll lose them. So go forth and apply your divinatory arts to dating, mating, and finding true love.

For Further Reading

RAFE ANDERSEN, *Total Palmistry, The Love Connection*, Red Wheel/Weiser, 2003.

SCOTT CUNNINGHAM, *Wicca: A Guide for the Solitary Practitioner*, Llewellyn, 1998.

DAVID FONTANA, *The Secret Language of Symbols: A Visual Key to Symbols and Their Meanings*, Chronicle Books, 1994.

MAC FULFER, *Amazing Face Reading*, self-published, 1996.

LINDA GOODMAN, *Love Signs*, Perrenial, 1992.

———, *Sun Signs*, Bantam, 1985.

STEPHEN LaBERGE, *Exploring the World of Lucid Dreaming*, Ballantine Books, 1991.

GLYNIS McCANTS, *Glynis Has Your Number: Master Your Relationships, Find the Right Career, and Discover What Life Has in Store for You!*, Hyperion, 2005.

RACHEL POLLACK, *Seventy-eight Degrees of Wisdom, A Book of Tarot*, HarperCollins/Thorsons, 1997.

Author Biographies

Stefanie Iris Weiss (RIGHT) and **Sherene Schostak** (LEFT) are New York City–based authors, astrologers, and best friends. They co-wrote *Surviving Saturn's Return: Overcoming the Most Tumultuous Time of Your Life* and are the astrology columnists for *Teen Vogue*. They're currently working on a book about male typology called *Just My Type*.

Stefanie Iris Weiss, M.A., is a writer, astrologer, and adjunct professor of writing. Her first novel for young adults, *Starrgazer*, is due out in 2006. She is the author of five self-help books, including, most recently, *Coping with the Beauty Myth: A Guide for Real Girls*. Her other books have covered topics as diverse as grief, yoga, and veganism. She has been teaching writing since 1998 and holds a Master's Degree in English Education from New York University.

Sherene Schostak, M.A., is a Jungian psychotherapist and astrologer in private practice for the past eleven years consulting, writing, and teaching. She is the creator of *Zodiac Dance: The Authentic Movement* DVD and the workshops from which it was derived. She holds a Master's Degree from New York University in Clinical Psychology and a Master's Degree in Psychoanalytic Studies from the New School for Social Research. Sherene also teaches classes and workshops internationally.